Financial Fitness for Life®

Student Workbook

Grades 6-8

Barbara Flowers
Sharon Laux
Authors, Second Edition

Barbara Flowers
Sheryl Szot Gallaher
Authors, First Edition

Teaching Opportunity®

AUTHORS, SECOND EDITION:
Barbara Flowers
Senior Economic Education Specialist
Federal Reserve Bank of St. Louis

Sharon C. Laux
Associate Director
University of Missouri - St. Louis Center for Entrepreneurship and Economic Education

AUTHORS, FIRST EDITION:
Barbara Flowers
Senior Economic Education Specialist
Federal Reserve Bank of St. Louis

Sheryl Szot Gallaher
Director
Governors State University, Office of Economic Education

PROJECT DIRECTOR:
Richard A. MacDonald
Senior Advisor for Program Development
Council for Economic Education
and
Assistant Professor of Economics
St. Cloud State University

PROJECT COORDINATORS:
Christopher Caltabiano
Vice President for Program Administration
Council for Economic Education

Irina Piven
Senior Program Associate
Council for Economic Education

EDITOR:
Richard Western

DESIGN AND LAYOUT:
Jill O'Leske
Impact Design, LLC

Presented by:

This publication was made possible through funding by the Bank of America Charitable Foundation.

ISBN 978-1-56183-695-6

5 4 3 2 1

Acknowledgments

AUTHOR SUPPORT TEAM:

Becky Forristal, Seventh Grade Teacher
Rockwood Valley Middle School
St. Louis, MO

Joseph G. Maiden, Seventh Grade Teacher
Fox Middle School
Arnold, MO

Melanie Vierling, Grades 6-8
L'Ouverture Middle Academy
St. Louis, MO

Kristen A. Wimbley, Sixth Grade Teacher
McKinley Classical Leadership Academy
St. Louis, MO

CONTENT REVIEWERS:

Kris Bertelsen
St. Charles High School
St. Charles, MN

Nathan Eric Hampton
St. Cloud State University
St. Cloud, MN

Scott Wolla
Federal Reserve Bank of St. Louis
St. Louis, MO

Table of Contents

Introduction

The Economic Way of Thinking

You've probably seen offers like the ones below in a store or in the mail. If companies are really willing to give products away for free, why do economists say "there is no such thing as a free lunch?" To answer this question, you have to understand that every choice involves a cost.

Because time, space, and money are limited, and human wants are unlimited, people cannot have everything they want. When people cannot have everything they want, they have to make choices, and when they make a choice, they must give something up. The next best alternative that is given up when a choice is made is the opportunity cost.

That's why there's no free lunch—or free CDs. There is always an opportunity cost.

When you make decisions, you need to consider, in a logical way, the opportunity cost of your choices. By using the economic way of thinking and by developing a good decision-making plan, you'll be able to evaluate your options and make better choices.

Resources Are Scarce

Introduction

What would you get if you won a $1 million lottery? Would that be more money than you could possibly ever spend? If you don't have $1 million, that might seem like a lot of money, and it is! However, it seems the common affliction among some lottery winners is that they burn through the money they have won nearly as fast as they obtained it. And that doesn't go only for the winners of a measly $1 million.

A quick look at the Internet will provide you with lots of examples of people who won big lottery prizes, just to be left in debt in a matter of a few years. The reasons are as numerous as there are things to buy. No matter how much you have, it's never enough.

Think of the wealthiest people among us. According to Forbes.com, Bill Gates generally places in the top two of wealthiest Americans. In 2008, his net worth was reported to be $57 billion. You might think that Bill Gates and his family could have everything they want. However, you would be wrong. Even Mr. Gates can't have everything he wants. Take a look at his foundation's website, www.gatesfoundation.org, and read the annual reports. You will find that Mr. Gates wants to provide a clean and sanitary environment in areas of the world where people have no clean water and no sewage system. He wants to eradicate HIV and malaria. He wants all public libraries to have the resources to provide computers and Internet access. He wants to provide job training for young people, and he wants to fund programs that will aid and support victims of domestic violence. The Bill and Melinda Gates Foundation has assisted programs that have made tremendous progress, but there are simply not enough resources in the world to meet all of the organization's wants.

Vocabulary

Capital resources: Man-made goods that are produced for the purpose of producing more goods and services.

Entrepreneur: A person who takes risk and gathers the resources to provide a new or improved good or service to the marketplace.

Human resources: People performing mental and physical work to produce goods and services.

Natural resources: Resources that occur naturally in and on the earth; these resources are used to make goods and services.

Productive resources: Basic resources used to produce goods and services: natural resources, human resources, capital resources, and entrepreneurial abilities.

NAME: ______________________ CLASS PERIOD: __________

Who Gets the Resources?

Your teacher will assign groups to portray the companies described below.

You own the **Maple Wooden Hat Company**. The hat is simply a bowl and a bill, similar to a baseball cap – only wooden. Unlike a baseball cap, your wooden hat is waterproof. It won't wear out like a baseball cap, and it can't be stained by sweat. And that's a good thing, because this hat is really hot. It doesn't fit most heads because, well, it's a bowl with a bill. These hats are expensive to produce, so you charge $35 per hat. Sales aren't very good. However, you're confident that these hats will gain in popularity. You want to build your inventory. You can buy wood for up to $10 per unit.	You own **Triple A Baseball Bat Company**. You noticed that high school leagues are returning to using wooden bats, so you got to work making the best wooden bats in the $30 price range. You anticipated there would be a market for wooden bats as kids moved into high school. Having used aluminum bats up until high school, they would now want to practice with wooden bats in preparation for their high school games. You have gained a strong market among individual players and among high school teams. You must replenish your dwindling inventory before January. You can buy wood for up to $30 per unit.
You own the **Fanciful Furniture Company**. You noticed that several makers of sofas and chairs were using upholstery fabrics in bright hues – oranges, yellows, blues, greens, even purples. You decided that this was an opportunity to make complementary tables in similar colors, so your coffee and lamp tables are painted various tints of orange, yellow, blue, green and purple. Sales are slow, so you would like to build more conventional tables. You can buy wood for up to $15 per unit.	Your company is **Buckingham Furnishings**. You make several very popular brands of furniture for sale in high-end and moderately-priced furniture markets. Your furniture is regularly featured in *Beautiful Home, Gorgeous Home,* and *Fantastic Home* magazines. With each new magazine issue, your sales skyrocket. You can't keep up with the demand for your furniture, so you are increasing the size of two of your plants to increase your production. You can buy wood for up to $30 per unit.
You own the **Premier Ashtray Company**. You got the idea when you were rummaging through your grandfather's attic and came across this intricately carved wooden tray. Although it was darkened with age, you could tell it had been beautiful. You've been producing similar pieces for the last year. Even though they are delicately carved and quite beautiful, your sales have been dismal. It seems that ashtrays aren't as popular as they were in your grandfather's day. You can buy more wood for up to $5 per unit.	You own the **Fold 'n Go Chair Company**. You make wooden folding chairs for outdoor use. You market your chairs as sturdy and strong. You've sold some, but it seems that people who take folding chairs to games and picnics prefer them to be light and easy to carry. Your chairs are heavy and cumbersome. You can buy more wood for up to $10 per unit.

EXERCISE 1.2

NAME: ______________________ CLASS PERIOD: __________

What Can Be Made Using...?

All resources are scarce and have competing uses, that is, any given resource might have several different uses. You've seen how wood can be used to produce many goods, which contributes to its scarcity. How about other natural resources, say water or land?

Your teacher will assign you and your group one natural resource from the list below.

Water **Oil** **One city block of land** **Ten city blocks of land** **Sand**

Write down as many uses for the resource as you can. Look around your classroom, think about the goods in your house, and think about the goods and services for sale in your neighborhood. Can you name 10 uses for your resource?

______________________ ______________________

______________________ ______________________

______________________ ______________________

______________________ ______________________

______________________ ______________________

______________________ ______________________

______________________ ______________________

LESSON 2

Making Decisions

Introduction

Back in your grandparents' day, corner grocery stores carried one or two brands of breakfast cereal, laundry detergent, and soft drinks. It was pretty easy then to decide what to buy with your hard-earned money.

Today's supermarkets and mega-malls are different; they offer thousands of choices. That's good because it provides variety in your life, but it also makes choosing more difficult.

When you go shopping, how do you decide what to buy? Do you pick the first box of cookies you see on a shelf? Do you simply choose the brand you've always bought, without checking out any new products? Or are you a careful shopper who compares ingredients and prices?

This lesson introduces you to a plan that will help you make decisions. The PACED decision-making process is a step-by-step strategy that you can use for making all kinds of choices—the right pair of jeans or basketball shoes, or the best way to spend your time on a Saturday night. Being able to make well-thought-out decisions will start you on the right path toward a lifetime of good choices.

Vocabulary

Alternatives: Options to be considered when making a decision.

Cost/benefit analysis: Comparing advantages and disadvantages in order to make a decision.

Criteria: Measures or requirements by which alternatives are judged.

Opportunity cost: The next-best alternative that is given up when a choice is made.

Trade-off: Giving up a little of one thing in order to get a little more of something else.

The PACED Decision-Making Process includes the following steps:

- State the **P**roblem.
- List **A**lternatives.
- Identify **C**riteria.
- **E**valuate Alternatives based on criteria.
- Make a **D**ecision.

Analyzing costs and benefits, as part of the PACED decision-making process, enables a person to make rational decisions. A rational decision is thought out and based on facts; the opposite would be an impulsive, spur-of-the-moment, emotional decision.

NAME: ______________________________ CLASS PERIOD: __________

Which Graham Cracker Is Best?

Use A, B, and C in the first column to identify your alternatives (different crackers).

List the characteristics by which you will judge the item across the top row (criteria).

Evaluate the alternatives using your criteria. Use the following scale for scoring:

1 = lowest (or worst) 2 = middle 3 = highest (or best)

Criteria → / ↓ Alternatives					TOTALS
A					
B					
C					

EXERCISE 2.2

NAME: ________________________________ CLASS PERIOD: ____________

Using the PACED Decision-Making Process

Read the following information about Marcus and Lydia. Then answer the questions and complete the grid following the second advertisement.

Marcus and Lydia each had $200, and each wanted to buy a new mp3 Player. They saw the following two ads in the newspaper for stores in a nearby shopping mall:

Party Time

$172.99

30GB 5th Generation Black mp3 Player

Video up to 2 hours of video playback

30 GB capacity

Holds up to 6,500 songs

Up to 14 hours of music playback

Up to 3 hours of slideshows with music

2.5-inch (diagonal) color LCD with LED backlight

4.8 oz.

Black finish

Audio output through headphone jack

Music Now!

$189.99

mp3 Player Classic 80GB Digital Multimedia Device

80GB capacity

Holds up to 20,000 songs

Up to 30 hours of music playback

1.5 inch color LCD with LED backlight

Voice recorder

4.9 oz.

Pink finish

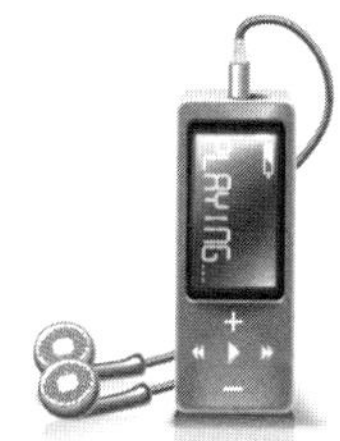

Questions and grid: Answer the questions and complete the grid as you work through the PACED process.

1. What is the problem? (List in the space above the grid.)

2. What are the alternatives? (List them in the first column.)

3. Name six criteria that Marcus and Lydia might consider when making their decision. (Put one in each cell in the row marked **criteria**.)

4. Evaluate the alternatives according to the criteria you listed, using "yes" or "no" in each cell.

5. Make a decision. What should Marcus and Lydia do? (List the decision in the space below the grid.) What is the opportunity cost of this decision?

Problem: ____

____

____

Criteria ➡ / ⬇ Alternatives						

What decision do you recommend? ______________________________

What is the opportunity cost of this decision? ______________________________

EXERCISE 2.3

NAME: ________________________ CLASS PERIOD: __________

Some Criteria Are More Valuable Than Others

The Noga Family decided it was time to get rid of their old desktop computer and buy a new laptop computer. They made a list of criteria that would be important in the choice they would make among various brands and models of laptops. After they compiled the list of criteria, they agreed that some characteristics of laptops were more important than others, so they gave more value to some criteria than to others. For example, having at least a 15-inch screen was more important to them than a built-in camera, and being "green compliant" was more important than having a minimum of a 2.5 hour battery life.

Here's how their criteria, as they valued them, looked in their PACED grid:

Criteria:	Values:
Under $1,000	5 points
15-inch screen or larger	4 points
Minimum of 2.5 hours battery run time	3 points
Green compliant	4 points
250 GB hard drive	4 points
Built-in camera	2 points

Read the following ads for six laptop computers. Then, using the PACED grid, help the Noga family decide which laptop computer will be the best choice, based on their criteria and the values they have assigned to their criteria.

1. Which computer should the Noga family buy, based on your grid?

____

2. Write a sentence or two explaining why the Noga family should buy the computer you suggested.

____

____

____

Laptop A **Buy it Today!** **$899**	Laptop B **Computer America** **Black and Silver** **$925**	Laptop C **Get it Now!** **$999**
Screen size 14.1″ Maximum battery run time 2 hours DVD writer Green compliant 160 GB hard drive Widescreen display High-speed processor Color: Titanium silver!	Built-in camera 1.3 megapixels Three USB ports WiFi link Battery run time 1.5 hours 250 GB hard drive Screen size 15″	Hot pink Two USB ports WiFi link Wide screen – 15″ Screen resolution 1280x800 Processor speed 2 GHz 160 GB hard drive Max battery run-time 4 hours! Case included
Laptop D **What a Buy!** **Go GREEN with Midnight Blue** **$999**	Laptop E **12-Month – No Interest!** **$899**	Laptop F **Close-out!** **Only ten left in store!** **$799**
Green compliant 250 GB hard drive capacity Screen size 15.4″ Maximum battery run time 3 hours Built-in camera	Black & Silver 160 GB hard drive 14″ screen 2 hours on battery power WiFi Auxiliary camera included Free case!	250 GB hard drive Green compliant 14″ screen 3 hour battery Free flash drive

Criteria ➡	Under $1,000	Minimum 15-inch screen	Minimum 2.5 hours battery run time	Green compliant	250 GB hard drive	Built-in camera	Total value
Value Alternatives	5	4	3	4	4	2	
A							
B							
C							
D							
E							
F							

NAME: ______________________ CLASS PERIOD: __________

Panel Discussion

Have you ever wondered how several groups, with similar information, can make different decisions about the same issue? It's probably because each group's criteria are different.

In Lesson 1, you noted several uses for an area of land. In this exercise, your group will evaluate land use based on criteria that are important to you. Then you will plan a panel discussion of the issue, based upon your group's concerns. (You can enhance your group's point of view by doing research, too.) In a political debate like this one, the side that gets the most votes wins; however, in this exercise it is not as important to win as it is to state clear and powerful arguments for your choice.

Your teacher will assign you to Group A, Group B, or Group C. Imagine that you are a person in that age group with the concerns listed on the group card. As a group, review your concerns and decide which position your group will support [i.e., (1) library and lab, (2) pool and recreation center, (3) senior-citizen housing facility]. Each person in your group should write a clear statement supporting one of the group's concerns (conducting extra research will help support your argument).

Issue

On 10 acres of vacant land, what should your town construct?

1. A library and computer lab?

2. A swimming pool and recreation center?

3. A senior-citizen housing facility?

____

____

____

____

____

____

GROUP A **Age 13-29**	GROUP B **Age 30-54**	GROUP C **Age 55-70**
Concerns: Year-round activities Athletic opportunities Health and fitness Social gatherings Organized competitive games	**Concerns:** Education Employment opportunities Access to information Investment reports Details about travel opportunities	**Concerns:** Retirement benefits Low-cost housing Contact with others of the same age Health care Companionship

After the groups have considered their criteria and applied them to the alternatives, each group will present a panel discussion to the class. Be sure to include information about the **alternatives** available, the **criteria** that are important to your group, your method of **evaluating the alternatives**, and your final **decision** for how the vacant land should be used. You may include posters, illustrations, charts, graphs, or a multi-media slide show to enhance your group's presentation.

When all the groups are finished, discuss the effectiveness of each group's arguments and their presentations.

LESSON 3

The Economic Way of Thinking

Introduction

Often, when you talk to a friend or relative, you learn about situations that make you scratch your head and ask, "Why would a person do this?" Here are some examples:

- A college student runs up $30,000 in credit card debt.
- A store marks down summer jackets from $300 to only $39.95 in October.
- Voters defeat a plan to finance a football stadium with property tax revenues.

Unlocking the secrets of these situations might be easier if you applied the economic way of thinking to determine WHY people act the way they do.

In this lesson, you will learn how to use the economic way of thinking, a process that can help you understand why people save, borrow, and spend the way they do. It will also help you make wise money decisions by examining the way you think and act.

Vocabulary

Consequence: The result or effect of a person's behavior.

Incentive: A reason or reward that motivates people to behave in predictable ways.

Opportunity cost: The next-best alternative that is given up when a choice is made.

NAME: ______________________________ CLASS PERIOD: __________

Every Choice Has an Opportunity Cost

Because of limited resources and unlimited wants, people have to make choices. Every choice has an opportunity cost. In each situation below, a person must make choices because time, space, and money are limited. Below each description, list the person's alternatives, the choice, and the opportunity cost.

1. Shaundra's mother's birthday is coming up. Shaundra would like to buy her mom a necklace, but the one she likes costs more than she has saved. What are Shaundra's alternatives? What will she do? What is her opportunity cost?

Alternatives ______________________________

____

Choice ______________________________

Opportunity cost ______________________________

2. Angelo wants to put a 50-gallon aquarium in his room. When he measured the room, Angelo discovered that he wouldn't have enough space for his flat screen TV and the aquarium. What are Angelo's alternatives? What will he do? What is his opportunity cost?

Alternatives ______________________________

____

Choice ______________________________

Opportunity cost ______________________________

3. Raul has raised $200 for a local charity. If he raises $15 more, he will be eligible for a raffle for a new computer. The raffle is tomorrow. What are Raul's alternatives? What will he do? What is his opportunity cost?

Alternatives ______________________________

____

Choice ______________________________

Opportunity cost ______________________________

NAME: ____________________ CLASS PERIOD: __________

Choosing the Better Incentive

This activity focuses on price, a powerful monetary incentive. Working with a partner, evaluate the pairs of coupons for the eight purchases below and, for each pair, choose the coupon that provides the greater cost savings. Then give the reason for your decision.

1. Book bag **$29.99 (buy one)** The better incentive is coupon #______ The reason is: ______________ ______________	1. Coupon: 20% off 2. Coupon: Save $5.00

2. Snappy-Krunch Cereal **$2.99 per box (buy three boxes)** The better incentive is coupon #______ The reason is: ______________ ______________	1. Coupon: Buy 2, Get 1 Free! 2. Coupon: Save $1.50 per box

3. Super-Nutty Peanut Butter **32 oz. jar for $2.56 or 48 oz. jar for $2.99 (buy two jars, either size)** The better incentive is coupon #______ The reason is: ______________ ______________	1. Coupon: Buy a 32 oz. jar at regular price, get another free! 2. Coupon: Save $0.50 on each 48 oz. jar

4. Soccer shoes **$69.95 a pair (buy two pairs)** The better incentive is coupon #______ The reason is: ______________ ______________	1. Coupon: Buy one pair, get another at half price! 2. Coupon: Two pairs for $100.00

5. Amusement park **All day admission ticket $45.00** **(buy 6 tickets)** The better incentive is coupon #________ The reason is: ________________________ __________________________________	1. Coupon: $5 off each ticket (limit 6) when you buy a case of root beer at $9.99 a case 2. Coupon: Buy 5 tickets at regular price, get the 6th one FREE

6. Scary movie festival **$8.00 each night for 6 nights** **(attend all 6 nights)** The better incentive is coupon #________ The reason is: ________________________ __________________________________	1. Coupon: 4 nights at regular price: half price the next 2 nights 2. Coupon: 5 nights at regular price - 6th night FREE

7. Pizza **$18.99 (buy 2 pizzas)** The better incentive is coupon #________ The reason is: ________________________ __________________________________	1. Coupon: Save $2.00 on each pizza. Limit 2 2. Coupon: Today only: 2 pizzas $35.00

8. Video game **$49.99 (buy 3 games)** The better incentive is coupon #________ The reason is: ________________________ __________________________________	1. Coupon: Rebate $14.00 each. Limit two. 2. Coupon: Save 20% no limit

NAME: ______________________________ CLASS PERIOD: __________

Using the Economic Way of Thinking

Directions: Read about the dance at Susan B. Anthony Middle School. Then respond to the questions.

Susan B. Anthony Middle School's Honor Society was planning a dance. A music committee decided to use a video-sound show for the dance, even though its price was $300 higher than the local DJ's price. By paying for the video-sound show, the committee members believed they could attract more students to attend the dance.

When the big night arrived, 250 students from a class of 300 attended the dance. It was the best rate of attendance any school dance had ever attracted. The Honor Society was pleased with the results of the fundraiser.

Questions

1. The committee could not choose both the DJ and the video-sound show. Why not? What was limited?

____

____

2. What did the committee choose?

____

____

3. What was the incentive for its choice?

____

____

4. What was the opportunity cost?

____

____

5. What were the costs and benefits of the choice?

____

____

6. List one or two consequences of the choice.

Write another decision-making story, along with questions like the ones above. Challenge your classmates to analyze your story, using the economic way of thinking.

NAME: ________________________ CLASS PERIOD: __________

The Economic Way of Thinking

A. Examine the decisions made by the people in the following situtations by using the economic way of thinking.

1. Instead of putting an extra $3,000 in their retirement fund, Florence and Joe decided to fly from Chicago to Florida for a week of golf and relaxation.

- Choice: ________________________
- Opportunity cost: ________________________
- Incentive: ________________________
- Suggest a consequence of their choice: ________________________

____

- How did Florence and Joe benefit from their choice? ________________________

____

2. Brian and Sheryl paid their credit card bill instead of making a down payment on a new convertible.

- Choice: ________________________
- Opportunity cost: ________________________
- Incentive: ________________________
- Suggest a consequence of their choice: ________________________

____

- How did Brian and Sheryl benefit from their choice? ________________________

____

3. Su-Zee, Lorena, and their friends went to the beach instead of working at the school book sale last weekend.

- Choice: ______________________________
- Opportunity cost: ______________________________
- Incentive: ______________________________
- Suggest a consequence of their choice: ______________________________

  ____
- How did Su-Zee, Lorena, and their friends benefit from their choice? ________

  ____

B. Use the economic way of thinking to explain "Why math teachers give homework every day." Consider that the teacher will have to correct the homework, and will have less time for other activities. Think of incentives and consequences for the teacher and the students that result from the teacher giving homework every day.

- Teacher's choice: ______________________________
- Opportunity cost: ______________________________
- Incentive for making the choice: ______________________________

  ____
- Suggest a consequence of the choice: ______________________________

  ____
- Who benefits? How? ______________________________

  ____

Introduction

Earning Income

There's an old saying that "great oaks from tiny acorns grow." The meaning is simple: great achievements begin small. Then they blossom and flourish.

Education and financial security are good examples of how this works in life. Doing well in the elementary grades, studying all through middle school, graduating from high school, and continuing your education are the little steps that usually result in a big payoff: an enjoyable job with a good income.

The best way to increase your chances for a good income in a career you enjoy is to begin planning NOW. Think about what you like to do in your spare time. Do you like to write stories, fix broken toys, play the trumpet, or gaze through a telescope? Don't worry if the things you enjoy are different from the activities your classmates find appealing. Everybody is unique. But by examining your options, and finding out about careers that will be in demand in the future, you'll be able to make choices that can lead to a good income in an occupation you truly enjoy.

LESSON

4

Why Stay In School?

Introduction

People do not work for money. They work for the goods, services, and security that money can buy. Of course, you'll be able to buy more of the things you want if you have more money. Besides working for the things money can buy, people also work for the personal satisfaction they gain from their work.

You can acquire money in several different ways. You could steal it—but that harms other people, and living in prison isn't too much fun. You can receive it as a gift—but that's not too steady or predictable. (Besides, your Aunt Mabel isn't going to send you a birthday check for the rest of your life.) If you're like most people, you'll get most of your money by working for it.

Working is something you'll probably do for 30, 40, or 50 years. So how can you make the most of your time on the job? The best thing to do is to plan ahead and invest in your human capital by getting as much education and training as possible, especially in a field for which you have an interest or aptitude.

By staying in school, learning a trade, earning an advanced degree, or serving an apprenticeship, you can master the skills and gain the knowledge you'll need to be successful in a career that you enjoy. Studies show that people with more education have more job satisfaction and earn higher incomes.

If you choose to stay in school you'll learn extra skills, become a more valuable worker, and have the opportunity to earn a higher income. With a higher income you'll have more opportunities to use the money you earn to plan for your financial future.

Vocabulary

Income: Money earned during a specific period (e.g., $10 per hour or $50,000 per year).

Marginal benefit: The additional benefit of one more unit of some good or service.

Opportunity cost: The next-best alternative that is given up when a choice is made.

Wages: Income earned from working.

NAME: ______________________________ CLASS PERIOD: __________

Some Things About School Are So ...

Finish the sentence "Some things about school are so ...," by listing those things about school you think are difficult or hard, those that are comfortable or so-so, and those that are easy for you.

Difficult	Comfortable	Easy

What actions can you take to improve your ability and skill in areas you find difficult?

____

____

What is your plan of action, your timeline, for improvement?

____

____

____

____

NAME: ______________________ CLASS PERIOD: __________

Steps to Success

Directions: Study the table below and answer the questions that follow.

Median Annual Earnings in 2009 Dollars by Levels of Educational Attainment	
Less than High School	$23,608
High School Graduate	$32,552
Associate's Degree	$39,572
Bachelor's Degree	$52,200
Master's Degree	$65,364

Questions

1. Based on the information in the table on page 26, calculate the difference in earnings between:

a. a high school dropout and a high school graduate: ______________________

b. a high school graduate and a graduate from a two-year college program (associate's degree): ______________________

c. a two-year college graduate and a four-year college graduate (bachelor's degree): ______________________

d. a four-year college graduate and an individual with a master's degree.
____

2. Based on the information in the table below, fill in the table by calculating years worked and lifetime earnings for a person at each level of educational attainment.

	HS dropout	HS diploma	Associate's Degree	Bachelor's degree	Master's degree
Annual Income	$23,608	$32,552	$39,572	$52,200	$65,364
Years worked					
Life earnings					

Source for both tables: Bureau of Labor Statistics Current Population Survey: http://www.bls.gov/emp/emptab7.htm. Data are 2009 annual averages for persons age 25 and over. Earnings are for full-time wage and salary workers.

For this exercise, assume that each person works until 70 years of age. Other assumptions include: a. the high school dropout begins full-time work at age 16; b. the high school graduate begins full-time work at age 18; c. the graduate of the two-year college begins full-time work at age 20; d. the graduate of the four-year college begins full-time work at age 22; e. the graduate with a master's degree begins full-time work at age 24.

LESSON 5

Choosing a Career

Introduction

Taryn Rose was in residency as an orthopedic surgeon. Her female patients would complain of foot pain that Rose associated with the high heels they were wearing. She had first-hand experience, often working 14 hour shifts wearing the same narrow, pointy-toed high heels. After a fruitless search for comfortable, yet stylish, shoes, Rose redirected her skills to shoe design. Tiki Barber, the New York Giants' MVP in 2000, 2002 and 2004, retired from football after the 2006 season. While still playing, Barber, along with his brother, Rondé, authored children's books. Since retirement, Barber has gone on to host *The Barber Shop* on Sirius Radio and work as a sports commentator for NBC. Alton Brown was working as a cinematographer and video director but had an interest in cooking. He found cooking shows on television boring and uninspired, so he enrolled in culinary school and created *Good Eats*, a quirky cooking show which now appears on the Food Network.

How could these people be so successful in such different careers? The answer is simple.

They all learned from their experiences and applied their expertise to new situations. Taryn Rose actually felt the pain her patients were going through and, with her medical knowledge, was able to design shoes that were both attractive and easy on the feet. As a professional football player, Tiki Barber used his experience to explain the nuances of football and other sports. Alton Brown blended his behind-the-camera experience and his knowledge of cooking to bring personality to a cooking show.

In any job, you have to solve problems, deal with different personalities and make customers feel special. Once learned, these lessons can be practiced in other occupations. Business millionaires such as Simon Cowell (S Records and *American Idol*), Jeff Bezos (Amazon.com) and Oprah Winfrey started out in ordinary jobs. Cowell was a clerk in a mailroom, Bezos flipped burgers, and Winfrey was a reporter. But their experiences taught them responsibility, dependability, and reliability. Later they were able to apply these and other acquired skills to new jobs, and eventually they became leaders in their companies.

You don't have to be rich and famous to recognize that the skills and experience you gain in one career can be utilized in another. In this lesson, you will learn how to examine and evaluate your own qualities so that you will be able to choose a path that will provide a variety of options for both job satisfaction and a good income.

Vocabulary

Career cluster: Jobs within a similar category, e.g.,artist and graphic designer, bookkeeper and accountant, chef and dietitian.

Entrepreneur: A person who takes the risk and gathers the resources to provide a new or improved good or service to the marketplace.

Human capital: Knowledge, skills, experience, and attitude that help a person do a job better.

Opportunity cost: The next-best alternative that is given up when a choice is made.

Productivity: The amount of output per unit of input; e.g., if 5 workers can produce 25 gizmos in one day, the productivity per day is 5 gizmos per worker.

SCANS Skills: Guidelines for workplace success (developed by the Department of Labor Secretary's Commission on Achieving Necessary Skills).

Self-assessment: Examining characteristics about yourself.

Work ethic: Determination and positive habits on the job. Positive habits include reliability, punctuality, friendliness, honesty, and ability to work independently or in cooperation with others.

EXERCISE 5.1

NAME: ______________________ CLASS PERIOD: ____________

Demand for Labor in Various Occupations

The chart on this page shows the Bureau of Labor Statistics' employment figures for 2006 and projected employment figures for the year 2016. Work with your teammates to calculate the number and percentage increase (+) or decrease (-) for each occupational area listed.

A: Industry	B: Actual # employed in 2006	C: Projected # employed in 2016	D: Change in number (Column C – Column B) indicate + or -	E: Percent change (Column D/ Column B) x 100 indicate + or -
Registered nurses	2,505,000	3,092,000		
Retail salespeople	4,477,000	5,034,000		
Customer service reps	2,202,000	2,747,000		
Food prep and serving	2,503,000	2,955,000		
Office clerks	3,200,000	3,604,000		
Personal & home care aides	767,000	1,156,000		
Home health aides	787,000	1,171,000		
Postsecondary teachers	1,672,000	2,054,000		
Nursing aides, orderlies	1,447,000	1,711,000		
Bookkeeping & accounting clerks	2,114,000	2,377,000		
Waiters and waitresses	2,361,000	2,615,000		
Child care workers	1,388,000	1,636,000		
Administrative assistants	1,618,000	1,857,000		
Computer software engineers	507,000	733,000		
Accountants and auditors	1,274,000	1,500,000		
Landscaping workers	1,220,000	1,441,000		
Elementary school teachers	1,540,000	1,749,000		
Receptionists and information clerks	1,173,000	1,375,000		
Truck drivers, heavy & tractor-trailer	1,860,000	2,053,000		
Maids and housekeeping cleaners	1,470,000	1,656,000		
Security guards	1,040,000	1,216,000		
Carpenters	1,462,000	1,612,000		
Management analysts	678,000	827,000		
Medical assistants	417,000	565,000		
Computer systems analysts	504,000	650,000		
Network systems analysts	262,000	402,000		
Teacher assistants	1,312,000	1,449,000		
Veterinarians	62,000	84,000		

EXERCISE 5.1

A: Industry	B: Actual # employed in 2006	C: Projected # employed in 2016	D: Change in number (Column C – Column B) indicate + or -	E: Percent change (Column D/ Column B) x 100 indicate + or -
Financial analysts	221,000	295,000		
Social & human service assistants	339,000	453,000		
Physical therapy assistants	60,000	80,000		
Pharmacy technicians	285,000	376,000		
Forensic science technicians	13,000	17,000		
Dental hygienists	167,000	217,000		
Mental health counselors	100,000	130,000		
Dental assistants	280,000	362,000		
Database administrators	119,000	154,000		
Physical therapists	173,000	220,000		
Manicurists and pedicurists	78,000	100,000		
Environmental science protection techs	36,000	47,000		
Physician assistants	66,000	83,000		
Stock clerks and order fillers	1,705,000	1,574,000		
Cashiers, except gaming	3,500,000	3,382,000		
Packers and packagers, hand	834,000	730,000		
File clerks	234,000	137,000		
Farmers and ranchers	1,058,000	969,000		
Order clerks	271,000	205,000		
Sewing machine operators	233,000	170,000		
Telemarketers	395,000	356,000		
Computer operators	130,000	98,000		
Word processors and typists	179,000	158,000		
Computer programmers	435,000	417,000		
Switchboard operators	177,000	163,000		
Tile and marble setters	79,000	91,000		
Plumbers, pipefitters, steamfitters	502,000	555,000		
Firefighters	293,000	328,000		
Medical equipment repairers	38,000	46,000		
Embalmers	9,000	10,000		
Nuclear medicine technologists	20,000	23,000		
Paralegals and legal assistants	238,000	291,000		
Cardiovascular technologists	45,000	57,000		
Interior designers	72,000	86,000		

NAME: ______________________________ CLASS PERIOD: ____________

Self-Assessment

The first step toward choosing a career that's right for you is to consider the things you like to do. Use the grid to assess characteristics about yourself. Then check the next page to learn how you can score yourself on this exercise.

Directions: Place a check (√) in the shaded box to the right of each statement that describes something you like to do. If you don't enjoy an activity, leave the boxes blank.

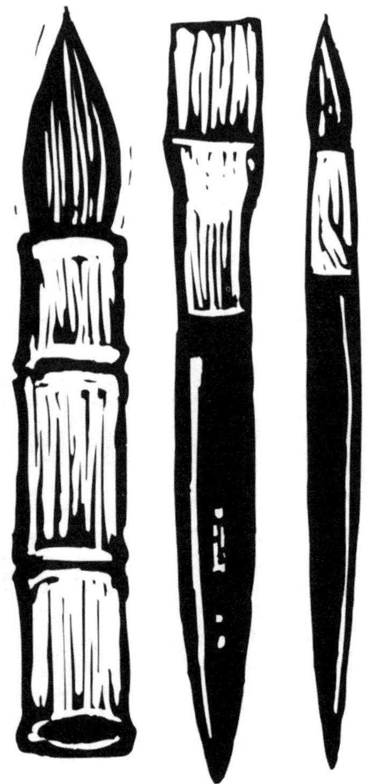

I like to:	1	2	3	4	5	6
fix electrical things						
play team sports						
sketch, draw, paint						
keep accurate records						
think abstractly						
write factual reports						
sell things or promote ideas						
play a musical instrument						
pitch a tent						
follow clearly defined procedures						
plan and supervise an activity						
be elected to office						
solve math problems						
work with numbers and data						
help people with problems						
write stories and poems						
attend concerts and art exhibits						
work outdoors						
use computers						
be responsible for details						
make decisions that affect others						
sing, act, and dance						
meet important people						
build things						
lead a group discussion						
do a lot of paperwork						
perform lab experiments						
use a miscroscope						
read fiction, plays, poetry						
give talks or speeches						
organize activities and events						
be physically active						
mediate disputes						
teach or train others						
work independently						

EXERCISE 5.2

So, what do your check marks mean? First, total the number of checks in each column, record them in this chart, and circle the top three. Then read the descriptions below:

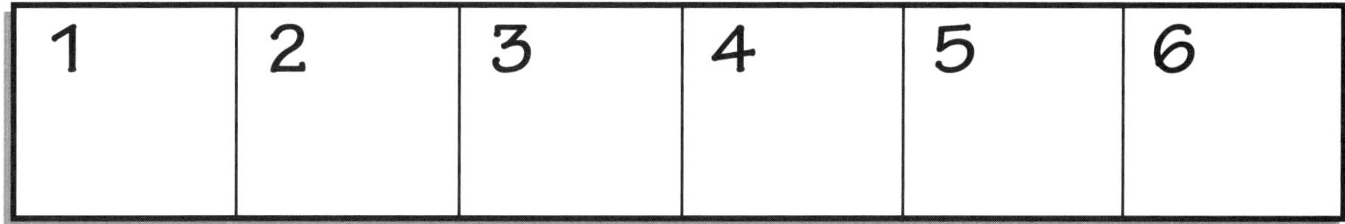

1	2	3	4	5	6

If one of your top three scores is in Box 1, you are interested in activities that require coordination or physical strength. You like to work with real problems instead of abstract ones. You're probably interested in scientific or mechanical areas.

If one of your top three score is in Box 2, you like to organize and understand things for yourself, but you're not interested in persuading others. You often enjoy working alone and are oriented more toward data and numbers than toward people.

If one of your top three scores is in Box 3, you value self-expression, dislike rigidity and structure, and are prone to be emotional. You are creative and artistic. You are probably interested in music, the fine arts, and crafts.

If one of your top three scores is in Box 4, you like to help people learn new things. You'd rather spend an evening talking with a friend than an afternoon playing basketball or skiing. You're a good listener and are interested in people. Friends often come to you for help in solving problems.

If one of your top three scores is in Box 5, you have keen verbal skills and like to use those skills to persuade others. You could probably be a good salesperson, advertiser, or politician.

If one of your top three scores is in Box 6, you don't mind rules and regulations, especially when you are in control. You enjoy order, and you like things to be organized. Messy things make you crazy. You are interested in tasks that require accuracy and precision.

Judging from your responses, prioritize the career clusters below.
(Number 1 is the cluster that is most appealing; Number 6 is the least appealing.)

Career Clusters	Typical Jobs
_____ Arts and communication	Actor, dancer, newscaster, stagehand
_____ Business & technology	Accountant, banker, travel agent
_____ Engineering & industry	Mechanic, medical technician, plumber
_____ Environmental science	Botanist, florist, marine biologist
_____ Health services	Aerobics instructor, dentist, veterinarian
_____ Human services	Cook, detective, judge, teacher

List the types of jobs that relate to the interests you identified in this self-assessment activity.

____

____

____

____

____

____

____

____

Adapted from the "Holland Occupational Themes" activity in the Self-Assessment Exercise at http://www.soicc.state.nc.us/soicc/planning/c1a.htm

NAME: ______________________________ CLASS PERIOD: __________

Human Capital and SCANS on the Job

Read the job requirements on the next page, taken from actual classified job ads. Then check which ads require the SCANS skills listed below. Write the numbers of the ads in the blanks. (All blanks will have more than one ad listed.)

______________ Basic skills (specific education requirements)

______________ Interpersonal skills (getting along with people)

______________ Teamwork

______________ Ability to use technology

______________ Good oral communication

______________ Problem solving

______________ Positive work ethic (good attitude)

______________ Experience

______________ Organizational skills

In the blanks below, write a short letter explaining why you should be considered for one of the jobs described in the ads. Be sure to include examples of how your human capital meets the requirements listed in the advertisement.

____

____

____

____

____

____

____

____

____

CLASSIFIED ADS

1. COMPUTER SYSTEMS ADMINISTRATOR
Leading metal company seeks an individual to be responsible for all aspects of network administration including servers, communications hardware, and software systems. Will plan, implement, and support the network and computing infrastructure. Will work with information technology group to maintain disaster recovery plans. Will develop documents, provide technical support, and conduct training.

Must have experience in computer networking. Excellent communication skills required, ability to learn/think independently.

Competitive benefits and salary.

2. HOTEL SALES MANAGER
Prestigious hotel is looking for an energetic manager to join our winning sales team. You will be responsible for selling and servicing small meetings in a fast-paced environment. The ideal candidate will have hotel background and be a highly motivated team player.

Excellent salary and benefits, including medical, dental, and 401K.

3. AUTO SALES
We're expanding our sales staff. We need motivated sales people with good communication skills and team spirit.

We offer commissions, bonuses, flexible hours, paid vacation, medical and dental plan, 401K and opportunities for advancement.

4. ADMINISTRATIVE ASSISTANT
Help design your own position. New warehouse needs someone to take charge of the phones and run the office. Must enjoy making order out of chaos, beating deadlines, and helping co-workers. Computer skills, pleasant disposition, and good sense of humor are required.

Full time. Good salary and benefits.

5. BIOLOGIST
Manufacturer of medical lab supplies seeks biologists. Responsibilities include project testing, interpreting and reporting test results.

You will investigate problems, recommend corrective actions, and develop new methods for testing existing products.

Must possess a degree in Life Sciences and have 3 years' experience. Competitive salary and benefits package.

6. RESTAURANT MANAGER
Oceanside Restaurant is searching for a Manager

Minimum of 3 years' experience in a luxury setting, excellent human relations and administrative skills. Must be able to accommodate guests in a gracious, sincere, timely and confident manner.

Superior benefits package including health, dental and life insurance, profit sharing, and 401K.

7. EDITORIAL COORDINATOR
You'll coordinate a team of editors and proofreaders assigned to a variety of projects. Must be a problem solver with strong team skills. Effective verbal and written communication is essential. Other responsibilities may include checking research and making corrections. You'll also update files, edit, and run reports.

PC and Mac experience a must. Excellent salary and benefits including 401K.

8. NETWORK MANAGER
Health Care Provider seeks someone to drive the development of a health network. Responsibilities include maintaining existing network, resolving health insurance claims, and educating patients about policies and procedures.

Must have a Master's Degree and 3 years' experience. Strong communication skills are expected. Word and Excel proficiency required. Some travel.

9. GRAPHIC DESIGN SUPERVISOR
Exciting opportunity for a detail-oriented individual with excellent organizational and communication skills. Job will include managing production and projects.

Quark, Photoshop and knowledge of Macintosh systems are a must. Must be able to coordinate many projects at one time.

Benefits include medical and dental insurance, profit sharing, 401K, and 30% employee discount.

10. CUSTOMER SERVICE REPRESENTATIVE
Manufacturer of bakeware seeks an experienced customer service rep. Candidate must have excellent phone skills, a positive attitude, and ability to solve problems on the spot. Must be proficient in Microsoft Word and have data entry experience.

Benefits include Medical/Dental/Vision Insurance, 401K plan and a fitness facility.

NAME: ______________________ CLASS PERIOD: __________

How Do Entrepreneurs Earn a Living?

You probably noticed that the job listings in Exercise 5.3 included information about salaries and benefits. Most people like having the security of a regular salary, paid health care insurance, and a retirement package. Entrepreneurs are different. When they take on the challenge of running their own business, they have to provide their own paychecks, insurance, and retirement plans. Consider the following situation.

Dimitrio is an entrepreneur. He quit his job at a local furniture store to open his own business. Being a talented woodworker, he handcrafts furniture to sell. He finds other items at auctions, repairs and resells them at a profit.

The figures below show how much Dimitrio earned each month when he worked as an employee at the furniture store. (For the sake of simplicity, taxes and Social Security are not included.)

Dimitrio's salary when he worked at the furniture store	$3,000.00
The value of Dimitrio's medical insurance	$300.00
The value of Dimitrio's dental insurance	$75.00
The value of Dimitrio's vision insurance	$75.00
The amount Dimitrio's employer contributed to his retirement	$60.00

The figures below show Dimitrio's July expenses in his new business.

Rent	$1,750.00
Electricity	$430.00
Heat	$370.00
Water	$215.00
Advertising	$1,200.00
Materials, supplies and equipment	$22,400.00
Maintenance and service of equipment	$350.00

A: Dimitrio had enough revenue in July to (1) pay his July expenses and (2) pay himself the same monthly salary and benefits he earned when he worked for someone else. How much revenue did Dimitrio earn in July?

____

B: If Dimitrio made the same amount of total salary and benefits running his own business as when he worked for someone else, should Dimitrio continue to run his own business?

____

BONUS: About what percent of total revenue did Dimitrio use to pay himself in July?

____

NAME: ______________________________ CLASS PERIOD: ____________

What's Wrong With This Picture?

Read the story below, and underline every statement that illustrates habits that will NOT prepare Kelly for a successful career. Then, above each incorrect statement, write the letter of the SCANS skill that Kelly is lacking. HINT: You should find more than 12 mistakes.

Choose from these SCANS skills:

- **A** Reading, writing and math
- **B** Interpersonal skills
- **C** Teamwork
- **D** Use of technology
- **E** Oral communication
- **F** Problem solving
- **G** Good work ethic/on time/good attitude
- **H** Organizational skills

Kelly is a seventh grader at Middleville Middle School. Her first class begins at 8:05, so she sets her alarm for 7:30. That way she's out of the kitchen door at 7:50 and ready for her 20-minute walk to school. Yesterday, when she entered the building, she saw the principal, Ms. Ramirez.

"Yo," Kelly shouted. "What's happenin'?"

"You're late, Kelly," said the principal, frowning.

"Whatever!" replied Kelly, and she raced down the hall.

In class, Kelly ruffled through her book bag but could not find any pens, pencils, or paper. When Mr. Choy asked for her math assignment, she didn't have that either.

"You'll have to go to the office," Mr. Choy told her.

In the principal's office, Kelly was asked to answer the phone while one of the secretaries stepped out. When the phone rang, Kelly picked it up.

"Hey, man, this is Middleville school. Whaddya want?" she said.

The caller hung up, but Kelly could not figure out why. She decided to leave a note for the secretary. It said: "Deer Sekretery, Somebody called and hung up. I don't no who it was."

When the phone rang again, Kelly said, "Whooze zis?"

"Please have Ms. Ramirez call the superintendent's office by 9:30," the caller said.

"Okay, okay," Kelly said. On a piece of scrap paper she wrote: "Ms. Ramirez - go to the custodian's office after 9:30."

"Kelly, you need to keep a good record of the calls," said the school clerk.

"You can't tell me what to do," shouted Kelly. "I'm doin' ya a favor by helpin' ya out."

The next day when Kelly woke up, it was dark in her bedroom. She flipped the switch about ten times, but her lamp would not light.

"Hey, what's wrong with my lamp?" she yelled to her mother.

"Maybe the bulb burned out," her mother suggested.

"Oh, I never thought of that," said Kelly.

Kelly had not done her homework, so she decided not to go to school. "Let's see, that's 15 days absent so far this year. That ain't too bad," she said.

When Kelly finally returned to school, her social studies teacher, Ms. Musielewicz, sent her to the computer lab to do some research for a big project. In the lab, Kelly was clueless. She did not even know how to turn on the computer. The lab assistant tried to help her, but Kelly just shrugged.

"I took that stupid computer class last year, but I didn't like it. Besides, I'm gonna be a mechanic when I'm done with school. I don't need no computer skills."

Finally, it was the last period of the day - gym class. The substitute teacher was assigning the students to teams for basketball. When Kelly got the ball, she dribbled down the floor and tried to shoot, even though she was surrounded by players from the other team.

"Pass. Pass the ball!" shouted the teacher.

But Kelly just tried to shoot again, and she was blocked by another player. Every time she got the ball, Kelly tried to shoot. She never passed to another player.

When the bell rang at the end of the day, Kelly grabbed her book bag and ran out of the building. On the way home she stopped at the store and bought a candy bar for 55 cents, giving the clerk a $1 bill.

"With tax, that's 59 cents. Your change is 31 cents," the cashier said, handing Kelly a quarter, a nickel and a penny.

"Hey," said another shopper, "That's not the right change."

"Sure it is," shrugged Kelly. "It must be. The man said it was."

When Kelly got home, her mother asked how things went at school. "All right, I guess," she replied. "But I can't wait to finish school and get a job. Then I can do anything I want."

Give Kelly some advice for how to improve her human capital and increase her chances for a successful career.

____

____

____

____

____

____

____

____

Productivity

Introduction

If you live in a city, you probably don't often think about the big changes that have taken place on U.S. farms. For example:

In 1950, the average U.S. corn farmer was able to harvest 39 bushels of corn from an acre of land. By the year 2009, that number had increased to 164.9 bushels.

Sources: National Agriculture Statistics Service http://www.nass.usda.gov
Productivity Growth in U.S., USDA Economic Research Service http://www.ers.usda.gov/publications/EB9/eb9.pdf

In 1950, the average amount of milk per cow was 5,314 pounds per year, but by 2009, this had increased to 20,848 pounds per year.

On average, each farmer in the year 2000 produced 12 times as much farm output per hour as farmers did in 1950.

Sources: National Agricultural Statistics Service
http://www.nass.usda.gov

Productivity Growth in U.S.,
USDA Economic Research Service
http://www.ers.usda.gov/publications/EB9/eb9.pdf

Technology has affected every area of productive resources. Productive resources are natural (soil, climate, minerals), human (people performance, mental and physical work), and capital (buildings, machinery and tools).

Look at how technology and education have affected productive resources:

Natural resources. Fertilizers, herbicides and insecticides, irrigation and crop rotation have increased the yield per acre of land.

Human resources. Farmers are educated today to use techniques and equipment that were unknown 100 years ago.

Capital resources. High-tech tools and machinery increase the output that farmers can expect from their fields and herds.

All these improvements mean more products for consumers: more steaks, hot dogs, pizzas, and, yes, more broccoli too. Increased productivity means that our standard of living is higher.

What does this have to do with the millions of people who don't live on farms? And what does it have to do with you?

Technology has not only affected farmers. Think about how your life has changed in the past few years because of new and improved tools. You can type a report quicker on a computer than on a typewriter; you can do research on the Internet at home without having to go to the library; you can order books and music CDs on-line instead of driving all the way to the mall.

That makes you more productive: you can accomplish the same amount of work in less time and with less effort. Someday you'll be able to use your new productivity and your improved human capital to get a better job, earn a higher income, and enjoy a higher standard of living for yourself and your family.

Vocabulary

Capital resources: Man-made goods that are produced for the purpose of producing more goods and services.

Human capital: Knowledge, skills, experience, and attitude that help a person do a better job.

Productivity: The amount of output per unit of input; e.g., if 5 workers can produce 25 gizmos in one day, the productivity per day is 5 gizmos per worker.

Wages: Income earned from working.

NAME: ______________________ CLASS PERIOD: __________

The Whole Story

A couple of years ago, Mike and Chris started a summer business.

It all started in February when the guys were talking about how they might earn some money. They were both 12, so they knew getting a job in a store or fast food place was out of the question because of their age. They decided to go into business for themselves.

After examining all the types of work typically done by boys their age, they decided to go into the grass-mowing business.

Chris went to work immediately. February and March are too early to cut grass, but he knew it wasn't too soon to start lining up customers. He printed flyers and went for long neighborhood walks, placing the flyers on the doorknob of every house he saw. He hung flyers on signs and trees. He placed ads in local papers and on bulletin boards at all the local stores.

When summer arrived, Mike and Chris had enough work to keep them busy 20 hours a week.

They cut grass all around the neighborhood. Chris even contacted Yolanda, the owner of the neighborhood ball field, and arranged to cut the field every Wednesday morning. The ball field was a good account; Chris had negotiated with Yolanda to get a fee of $16.00 per hour ($8.00 per person).

Week after week, Mike and Chris cut the grass at the ball field. They had identical lawn mowers, began cutting at the same time, and finished in two hours. However, at the end of each two-hour work session, Mike had cut three-fourths of the field while Chris had cut only one-fourth. Yolanda commended Mike for his productivity.

It may have been that Mike was simply a better worker than Chris; however, there may have been other differences that affected the boys' productivity.

A: What skills did Chris have that Mike maybe did not have?

____

____

B: Was Mike really more productive than Chris was? Why or why not?

____

____

NAME: ______________________________ CLASS PERIOD: ____________

Career Search

Choose a career that interests you.

For example, you might be curious about a career in web design, biological research, public relations, or health care. Even though your first full-time job may seem a long way off, it's never too early to begin to prepare. Find two articles from a popular magazine, a website, or newspaper that feature a career that interests you. You may substitute an interview with someone currently in your career choice for one of the articles. Use the information in the articles and interview to answer the following questions. Attach a copy of the articles or interview to this sheet.

On what career are you focusing?

____

What do you find interesting about this career?

____

____

What capital resources might someone use in this career?

____

____

In what ways does the use of these capital resources help the worker to be more productive?

____

What skills are required of someone in this career?

____

What level of education would you need to acquire the skills for this career?

____

What subjects, in particular, would you need to study?

____

What is the average annual salary for someone in this career?

____

Introduction

Money Management

When writing an article, newspaper reporters are taught to answer these questions: Who? What? Where? When? How? Why? You've probably been told to think about those same questions when you study for a science or social studies test, or when you analyze a novel or short story. The W and H Questions can help you make sense of important information, and they can also apply to financial matters.

Who? Of course, it's you!

What? Learn how to manage money

Where? Bank, credit union, savings and loan, stock market, Internet, newspapers, magazines

When? The sooner, the better; right now is a good time to start

How? Spending, planning, saving, investing

Why? To prepare for a secure financial future

LESSON 7

Managing Cash

Introduction

Every year, many families spend hours and hours planning a vacation. They look through travel brochures and check Internet websites. They do research at their local libraries; they ask friends, relatives, and professional travel agents for suggestions. Then they sit down with maps and itineraries, planning the routes they'll take and the sites they'll visit. They might even make reservations months in advance. They know from experience that the better their plan, the more likely they are to have an enjoyable time.

Being a good money manager requires planning too. The good news is that you don't have to be a professional to be good at it. Just as families learn from their previous vacation experiences, you can review the strengths and weaknesses of your past spending decisions. Just as travel agents draw routes and select highways to specific end points, you can map out your goals for financial success. These goals become the foundation for your spending plan, which is a statement of your projected income and expenses. Then, when your spending plan is in place, you'll be ready to save and spend responsibly. Of course, just as an unexpected detour means a change of plans on a vacation, unforeseen circumstances may cause you to adjust your spending plan. For example, your class trip may cost more than you expected, or you may have to get a new band uniform. That's when an emergency fund comes in handy.

In this lesson, you will learn how to design a spending plan. You will start by examining your expenses; then you will evaluate your income. Being able to keep your expenses lower than your income will help you meet short-term goals now. More important, sticking to a sensible spending plan is a skill that you will use as you work to achieve long-term goals for your future.

Vocabulary

Fixed expenses: Expenses that cannot be easily changed and that remain essentially the same from month to month (e.g., monthly car loan payment).

Occasional or periodic expenses: Expenses that occur once or a few times a year (e.g., birthday gifts, personal property tax).

Opportunity cost: The next-best alternative that is given up when a choice is made.

Periodic income: Income not earned on a regular schedule (e.g., occasional baby-sitting, summer jobs, gifts from relatives).

Planned expense: Spending you expect and for which you plan.

Spending plan: A plan for managing income and expenses.

Trade-off: Giving up some of one thing in order to acquire more of another.

Unplanned expense: Spending for an emergency, an urgent need, or an impulse purchase.

Variable expenses: Expenses that can be controlled and that change from month to month (e.g., restaurant meals).

NAME: ______________________________ CLASS PERIOD: __________

Keeping Track of Cash Flow

Have you ever spent a day at the mall with your friends and wondered where all your money went? You may have started the day with $50 in your wallet and found, by 8 p.m., that you didn't even have enough cash for a burger and fries at the food court. What happened?

Money has a way of getting spent—a little bit here, a little bit there—almost on its own. You'll probably be surprised to see how a little bit here and a little bit there can add up to a lot of spending in just a week.

Use the expenses chart below to record every expense you have for a week. Indicate whether the expense is for Food (F), Clothing (C), Entertainment (E), or Other (O) by placing the amount you spend in the appropriate column. Also note if the expense was planned (PL) or unplanned (UN), and identify each expense as Fixed (FX) or Variable (VR). If you need more space, set up a separate sheet of paper in the same way.

After you have kept this record of expenses for one week, total each column with numbers. This tells you how much you spent in each category. Then add those figures together for a grand total. Use the grand total to calculate the percent spent for each category. Count up how many expenses were planned and how many were unplanned. Do the same for the fixed and variable expenses. Now you are ready to answer the questions on the next page. Note: You may wish to set up a computer spreadsheet to help you with the record keeping.

Date	Item/ Service	(F) Food	(C) Clothing	(E) Entertainment	(O) Other	(PL) or (UN)	(FX) or (VR)
3/1	Snacks	3.53				UN	VR
Totals							
Percent							
Grand Total (F+C+E+O) =							

EXERCISE 7.1

Use the information from your expenses chart to answer these questions:

1. For which of your expenses did you plan ahead of time?

2. Which expenses were unplanned—that is, bought on the spur of the moment?

3. If you had the week to do over, which expenses would you change? Explain.

4. Which unplanned expenses were bad decisions? Explain.

5. Which unplanned expenses were good decisions? Explain.

6. Which sort of expense would be the easiest to decrease—fixed or variable?

7. Which of the expenses would be easiest for you to decrease if you needed money for an emergency purchase?

NAME: ____________________ CLASS PERIOD: __________

Living Within Their Means

Read one of the case studies on this or the following pages and decide whether the person kept his or her income and expenses in balance. (Note: All incomes are after income taxes have been paid.) Then answer questions 1-4 at the end of the exercise, and report your answers to the class. After each group gives a report, answer questions 5-9.

Case Study A

Lauren earns $51,300 a year as a teacher in a booming suburban school district. She has the following monthly expenses:

Contribution to retirement plan	$240
Rent/home mortgage	780
Utilities	340
Phone/cable/Internet	180
Food/groceries	300
Car payment	660
Insurance (car/rental/home)	188
Transportation, incl. gas	168
Charity	92
Clothes	66
Loan payments	540
Entertainment	240
Services (cleaning, hair dresser)	180
Other	166

Did Lauren spend more or less than she earned? ____________________

____

By how much? ____________________

Case Study B

Brian earns $42,000 a year by operating his small business. He has the following monthly expenses:

Contribution to retirement plan	$222
Rent/home mortgage	870
Utilities	288
Phone/cable/Internet	210
Food/groceries	290
Car payment	438
Insurance (car/rental /home)	178
Transportation, incl. gas	105
Charity	107
Clothes	138
Loan payments	368
Entertainment	180
Services (cleaning, hair dresser)	150
Other	222

Did Brian spend more or less than he earned? ____________________

____

By how much? ____________________

Case Study C

Maria is a pre-med student, but she works part-time as a lab assistant at the university. She earns $44,000 a year and has the following monthly expenses:

Contribution to retirement plan	$120
Rent/home mortgage	690
Utilities	342
Phone/cable/Internet	270
Food/groceries	450
Car payment	150
Insurance (car/rental/home)	264
Transportation, incl. gas	96
Charity	24
Clothes	222
Loan payments	728
Entertainment	198
Services (cleaning, hair dresser)	90
Other	180

Did Maria spend more or less than she earned? ____________________

____

By how much? ____________________

Case Study D

Suzanne is the executive vice president of a Silicon Valley computer engineering firm. She earns $160,000 a year and has the following monthly expenses:

Contribution to retirement plan	$1,780
Rent/home mortgage	4,804
Utilities	670
Phone/cable/Internet	324
Food/groceries	336
Car payment	900
Insurance (car/rental/home)	750
Transportation, incl. gas	450
Charity	670
Clothes	270
Loan payments	900
Entertainment	540
Services (cleaning, hair dresser)	438
Other	306

Did Suzanne spend more or less than she earned? ____________________

____

By how much? ____________________

Case Study E

Marcus is an attorney working as a prosecutor in a small town in Iowa. He earns $80,400 a year and has the following monthly expenses:

Contribution to retirement plan	$780
Rent/home mortgage	1,529
Utilities	342
Phone/cable/Internet	114
Food/groceries	409
Car payment	420
Insurance (car/rental/home)	225
Transportation, incl. gas	102
Charity	114
Clothes	180
Loan payments	1,661
Entertainment	342
Services (cleaning, hair dresser)	114
Other	324

Did Marcus spend more or less than he earned? ________________

____

By how much?________________

Case Study F

Jeff is a successful superintendent for a small construction company in Texas. He earns $40,400 a year and has the following monthly expenses:

Contribution to retirement plan	$240
Rent/home mortgage	900
Utilities	78
Phone/cable/Internet	54
Food/groceries	336
Car payment	186
Insurance (car/rental/home)	138
Transportation, incl. gas	168
Charity	66
Clothes	48
Loan payments	714
Entertainment	54
Services (cleaning, hair dresser)	72
Other	90

Did Jeff spend more or less than he earned? ________________

____

By how much?________________

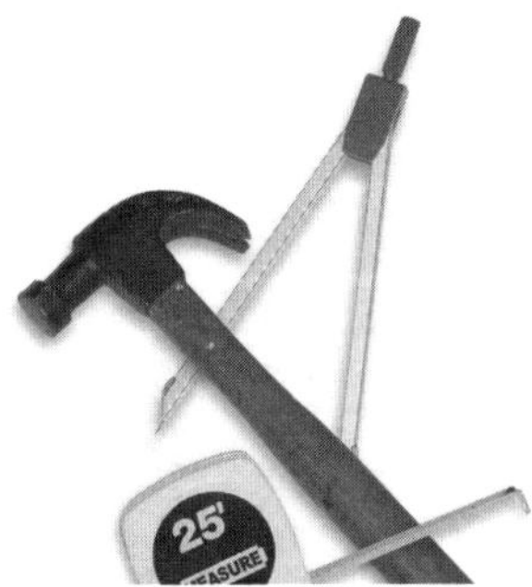

EXERCISE
7.2

Respond to the following questions about the person whose case study your group analyzed:

1. The person's car needs a new timing belt at a cost of $840. What changes would you make in his or her spending plan?

2. What are some of the trade-offs the person will face as a result of the choices you made above?

3. What was the person's monthly income?

4. Make some suggestions for how the person whose case study you read could budget his or her income and expenses more wisely.

Exchange information with other teams in your class to answer these questions:

5. Who had the most money left at the end of the month?

6. Who overspent the spending plan?

7. Which workers had between $100 and $200 left at the end of the month?

8. How much income did Marcus have left over at the end of the month?

9. If Lauren chooses to take a trip this month that costs $600, what are some trade-offs she'll have to consider?

NAME: ________________________ CLASS PERIOD: ____________

A Budget for a Secret Agent

Evaluate the spending plan of James Bond, double-agent and all-around cool guy. Use the income and expense information given, and analyze his money-management skills.

Income

Annual salary (take-home, net)	$1,575,654
Bonus for apprehending spies (net)	65,000
Gifts from foreign dignitaries (net)	14,000
Auto, meals, travel and clothing allowance	320,000
TOTAL INCOME	________

Expenses

Retirement plan	$165,987
Restaurant meals	82,999
Airplane tickets	89,454
Auto cost and maintenance	87,500
Clothing	75,009
Concert tickets	5,367
Opera tickets	4,389
Ballet tickets	3,567
Furniture	76,456
Oil paintings	235,643
Yacht and maintenance	132,654
Private plane and maintenance	354,762
Maintenance of home in France	113,231
Maintenance of home in Colorado	97,543
Maintenance of home in Hawaii	175,432
Charity	274,123
TOTAL EXPENSES	________

1. Are James Bond's expenses (**<** , **=** , **>**) his income? (Circle the right answer.)

2. If Bond decides to buy a new plane for $175,000, what is his opportunity cost?

   ____

3. Bond's financial advisor has said he should save 15% of his income; how much is that?

   ____

4. If Bond follows the advice of his financial advisor, what are some trade-offs he'll have to consider?

   ____

Choosing and Using a Checking Account

Introduction

Buying a new mp3 player is not a snap decision. You have to know the storage capacity of the player – the larger the capacity, the more music and video you can store. How easily can you download and then find the music you want to hear? Does the player use rechargeable batteries? How many hours of play do you get before you have to replace or recharge the batteries? Does the player have an FM tuner? Sometimes it's nice to listen to the radio.

In addition, you have to think about how you will use the mp3 player. If you jog, you will want a lightweight flash memory-based player that isn't bothered by jarring. If you want lots of storage and high quality sound, a high capacity hard-drive model will be best for you.

If you analyze how you'll use your mp3 player and check out lots of options before you buy, you'll most likely choose the one that's best for you. Deciding on the right checking account (at a bank, savings and loan, credit union, etc.) is somewhat like deciding on the right mp3 player. You need to know what's available and how you'll use it.

This lesson introduces you to checking accounts. You'll learn about the advantages and disadvantages of a checking account, as well as how to open and use one sensibly. By making sound decisions (either for an mp3 player or for where to put your hard-earned money), you'll be well on your way to a future of financial security.

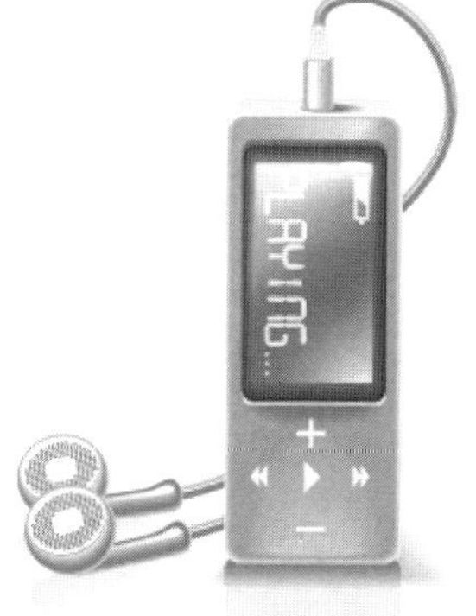

Vocabulary

ATM: Automatic teller machine.

Debit card: A plastic card that is used to deduct funds automatically and immediately from a checking account.

Deposit: Adding money to a bank account.

FDIC: Federal Deposit Insurance Corporation. Institutions that have an FDIC designation currently guarantee your bank deposits up to $250,000.

Interest: Money paid for the use of someone else's money.

Overdraft: Writing a check or using a debit card for an amount that is more than the amount on deposit in a bank account.

PIN: Personal Identification Number; a confidential code used to access private financial information or to make a transaction.

Service charge: The fee charged by a financial institution for certain services it provides to customers.

Smart card: A plastic card with a microchip that both stores and transfers information. These cards can be used for identification and as either a credit or debit card.

Withdrawal: Subtracting money from a bank account.

EXERCISE 8.1

NAME: ______________________ CLASS PERIOD: ____________

Design a Check

You've probably handled a check or two. Could you reproduce a check without looking at one? Use the following area to design a check. Be sure to include all of the information provided on a check.

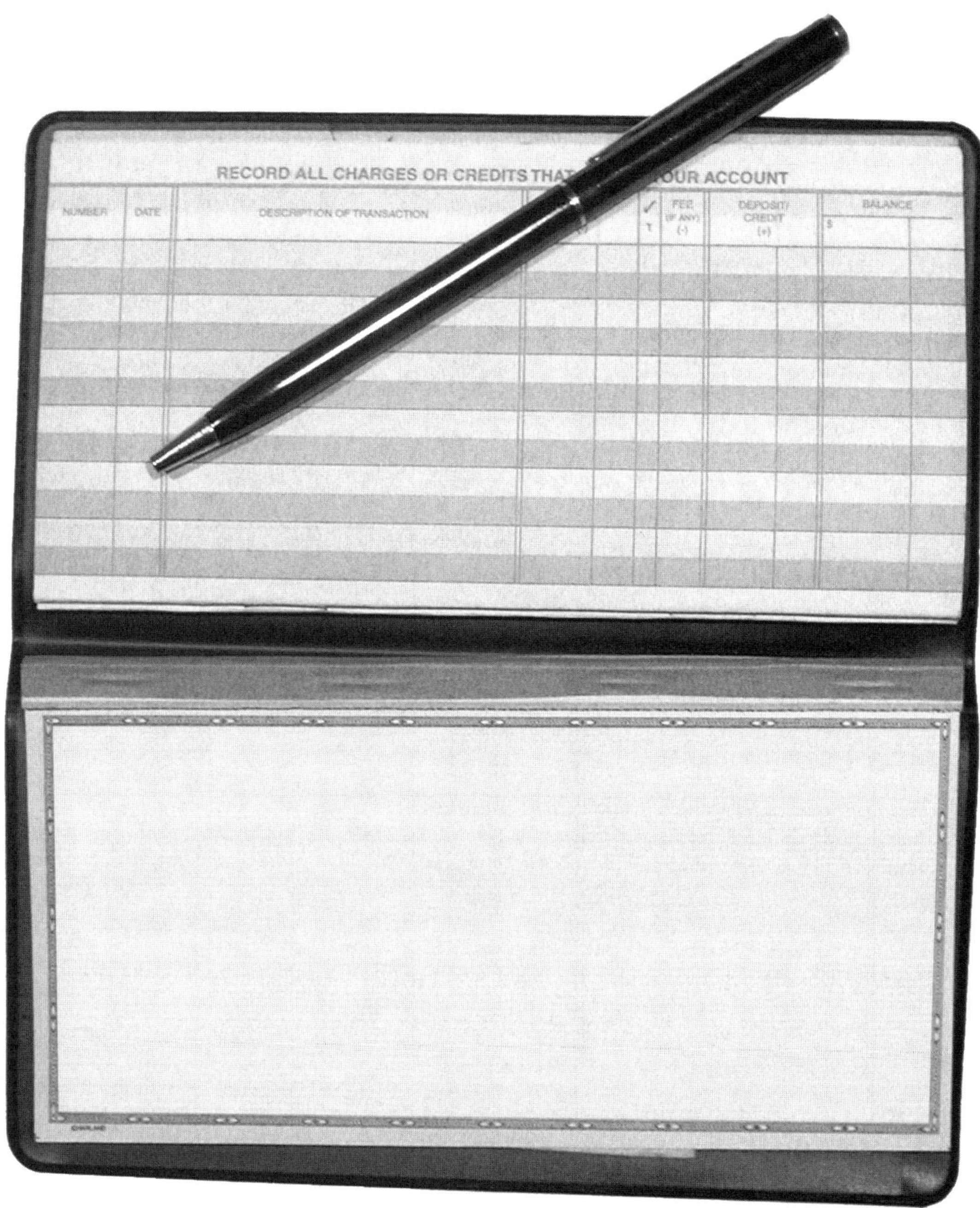

NAME: ______________________________ CLASS PERIOD: __________

Using a Checking Account

Starting with a beginning balance of $172.52, complete the checkbook register with the following transactions. Use Visual 8.3, Write a Check (which is provided by your teacher), and the blank checks on the following page to write checks for the transactions below that involve a payment by check.

Sept. 4	Used debit card to download an album for $10.
Sept. 8	Deposited paycheck for $83.46 from part-time job.
Sept. 11	Used debit card for $24.50 oil change at Grayson's Service Station.
Sept. 15	Used debit card for $15.00 as deposit for class ring at Acme Jewelers.
Sept. 19	Stopped by ATM to withdraw $40 cash.
Sept. 22	Deposited paycheck for $63.88.
Sept. 23	Wrote check #8455 for $5.00 to Lee Johnson to pay back borrowed money.
Sept. 26	Wrote check #8456 for $16.50 to American Publishing for subscription.
Sept. 27	Wrote check #8457 for $33.63 to Neighbor's Store for mother's birthday gift.
Sept. 29	Deposited $12.00 earned for baby-sitting.
Sept. 30	Automatic withdrawal of $56.96 from checking account for monthly auto loan payment.
Oct. 1	Monthly statement showed a service charge of $5.90 was debited from account.

PLEASE BE SURE TO DEDUCT CHARGES THAT AFFECT YOUR ACCOUNT

CHECK #	DATE	TRANSACTION DESCRIPTION	WITHDRAWAL/ TRANSACTIONS		✓ T	FEE IF ANY	DEPOSIT/ ADDITIONS		BALANCE	
		Starting balance							$172	52

EXERCISE 8.2

Blank Check Foundation
123-457-7891
23 W. Blank Check St.
New York City, New York

90-29304/2934
1930000000

CHECK No. 8455

DATE ____________

PAY TO THE ORDER OF ______________________ $ [ ]

______________________ DOLLARS

MyBank USA
123-457-7891
19204 W. Blank Check St.
New York City, New York

MEMO / NOTES: ____________ SIGNATURE: ____________

⑆823949 92999 3939⑆ 2384829 9290⑈ 8455

Blank Check Foundation
123-457-7891
23 W. Blank Check St.
New York City, New York

90-29304/2934
1930000000

CHECK No. 8456

DATE ____________

PAY TO THE ORDER OF ______________________ $ [ ]

______________________ DOLLARS

MyBank USA
123-457-7891
19204 W. Blank Check St.
New York City, New York

MEMO / NOTES: ____________ SIGNATURE: ____________

⑆823949 92999 3939⑆ 2384829 9290⑈ 8456

Blank Check Foundation
123-457-7891
23 W. Blank Check St.
New York City, New York

90-29304/2934
1930000000

CHECK No. 8457

DATE ____________

PAY TO THE ORDER OF ______________________ $ [ ]

______________________ DOLLARS

MyBank USA
123-457-7891
19204 W. Blank Check St.
New York City, New York

MEMO / NOTES: ____________ SIGNATURE: ____________

⑆823949 92999 3939⑆ 2384829 9290⑈ 8457

About Checking Accounts

A checking account provides certain benefits:

- Using checks or a debit card is safer than carrying cash or mailing cash.
- It makes day-to-day money transactions easier to handle.
- It can be less expensive than using money orders or check-cashing services.
- It provides a good record of purchases or expenditures. Copies of paid checks serve as proof of payment. Monthly statements track where money was spent.
- It helps people establish a good financial record with a financial institution.
- Online banking is a convenient way to pay bills.

Checking accounts come with certain features and costs. Be sure to ask the following questions:

- Does the account pay interest? If so, what balance is required to earn interest?
- Are there monthly service charges and/or per-check or debit card use charges?
- What are the fees for such items as printed checks, use of the ATM and debit cards, overdrafts (check written without sufficient funds in account), and stop payment services (request by a depositor for the bank not to pay a check that he or she has written)?
- Is there a "free checking" account? What are the requirements for such an account?

If you open a checking account, you take on certain responsibilities. It is your responsibility to:

- Protect your checkbook, debit card, or ATM card to guard against theft.
- Write checks correctly to prevent tampering or forgery.
- Keep a running total and balance your account monthly to avoid overdrafts.

Opening a Checking Account

1. Financial institutions vary in the types of checking accounts they offer. Choose a financial institution that offers a checking account that you believe is best for you and is convenient for you to use.

2. Take identification to the bank officer handling new accounts. Make sure to take a copy of your driver's license, an official state identification card, or a birth certificate, as well as your Social Security number. If it is to be a joint account, bring information for the second person as well. A joint account will give the other individual equal access to the money in the account. Financial institutions usually require a parent or another adult to be named on the account (joint account) if you are under 18 years old.

3. Provide the bank officer with information, including:
   - Current address and phone number. This is so the bank knows where to send your monthly statement and how to reach you if there are questions.
   - Social Security Number, mother's maiden name, and your birthplace. This provides the bank with information that only you know, so that you are protected in case someone tries to use, or seek information about, your account.

4. Complete a signature card. The bank will keep this card as a sample of your signature to protect against unauthorized individuals using your account. If you select an interest-bearing account, you will be asked to sign a W-9 Form, which will allow the bank to pay interest without withholding tax.

5. Make an opening deposit. You will need to deposit at least the minimum amount required by that financial institution.

6. Read and review the disclosures that the bank officer will give you. These are important materials that cover such areas as how interest is paid on an interest-bearing account, how to order checks, how to set up and use an ATM and debit card, and other rules about the account.

Ten Tips for ATM, Debit, and Online Safety

1. Stay alert. Be aware of your surroundings when you use an ATM, especially at night. It's best to use an ATM only in a well-lighted area and to have someone accompany you.

2. Report suspicious activity. If you notice anything unusual, cancel your transaction, pocket your card, and leave immediately. Go to a safe place and call the police if you suspect dangerous or illegal activity.

3. Be prepared. To complete your transaction safely, fill out your account deposit forms and have your card ready before arriving at the ATM. When you've completed your transaction, pocket your card, receipt, and cash immediately. It is unwise to count cash openly in front of others.

4. Take special precautions at drive-up ATMs. When using a drive-up ATM, remember always to keep your car doors locked, all other windows rolled up, and the car running.

5. Treat your debit card like cash. Guard your debit card as carefully as you do cash, checks, and credit cards. Never give account numbers, card information, or your personal identification number (PIN) over the phone.

6. Keep your PIN and passwords secret. Don't write them on your card or keep them in your wallet. Memorize your number and do not tell anyone what it is, not even family members and bank employees.

7. Be courteous while waiting at an ATM. Keep a polite distance from the person using the ATM before you. Allow that person to complete the transaction before you approach the machine.

8. Protect your privacy. Be mindful of others waiting behind you. Position yourself in front of the ATM keyboard to prevent someone from observing your PIN. When banking online, look for the encryption icon (a lock or key) on your screen to be sure your information can't be read by others. Try to avoid using wireless connections for financial transactions.

9. Save your ATM and debit card receipts. Remember to record each transaction in your checkbook register and match it to your monthly statement. Protect your receipts. They may contain confidential information.

10. Report a lost or stolen card immediately. Call the bank as soon as you realize your card has been lost or stolen so the bank can cancel your lost card and begin the process of issuing you a new card. The telephone number to call is usually listed on your statement.

NAME: ________________________________ CLASS PERIOD: __________

What's Great About Our Checking Accounts

As the new public relations manager for a local bank, you've been asked to develop an advertisement stating the virtues of your bank and the checking accounts it offers. Contact a local bank, savings and loan, or credit union by phone or online to gather information on the available checking accounts. In your ad, be sure to highlight strengths of the financial institution, such as location and banking hours, and the specific features of the accounts it offers. Use the following list of features and costs to develop your advertisement.

Checking Account Features and Costs:

- Monthly fees
- Minimum balance needed to avoid paying a monthly fee
- Availability and cost of online checking and bill paying
- Per-check charges
- Penalty fees for overdrafts
- Debit card/ATM charges
- Stop-payment fees
- Charges for printed checks
- Availability of overdraft protection
- Interest rates on interest-bearing accounts

LESSON 9

What Taxes Affect You?

Introduction

Everybody likes to drive on smooth roads and enjoy the beauty of national parks. Everybody wants good schools, safe neighborhoods, and clean streets. Everybody wants to enjoy these benefits, but who pays for them?

You have already learned that every benefit has a cost. The cost of highway construction and forest maintenance or police and fire protection is high. Where does the money come from to pay for the resources necessary to maintain beauty and safety in your city, your state, or the whole United States?

If you answered taxes, you're correct. Different kinds of taxes are used to fund the projects that citizens want. For example:

- Property (real estate) taxes help pay for local schools.
- Federal income taxes are used to fund our national defense programs.
- State income taxes go toward parks and social services.
- Local sales taxes pay for the upkeep of libraries.
- Payroll taxes pay for Social Security and Medicare benefits.

Vocabulary

FICA: Federal Insurance Contributions Act (a payroll tax that is commonly called Social Security). This is a transfer tax because it (indirectly) transfers money from people who are working to those who no longer work and are eligible to receive Social Security, Medicare, or disability payments.

Gross pay: Total earnings for total hours worked.

Income tax: A tax on earnings; every worker who earns a certain amount must pay federal income taxes. (Most states and some cities also have their own income taxes.)

IRS: Internal Revenue Service; the agency that collects federal income taxes.

Net pay: Amount of earnings received after all deductions (including taxes) have been taken into account.

Payroll deduction: Amount of money automatically subtracted from gross pay for taxes, insurance, retirement benefits, etc.

Real estate property tax: A tax paid by people who own homes, business properties, condominiums, or other real estate. Property tax may also be charged on personal property, such as boats or cars.

Take-home pay: Same as net pay.

Transfer payments: Payments by government to people who do not currently perform productive services.

Is This a Road or a Parking Lot?

Tony's family owned a hardware store in town. The store was established nearly 75 years ago by Tony's great-grandparents. As a child, Tony would visit his great-grandparents who lived in an apartment above the store. For his great-grandparents, it was a convenient place to live; they could simply walk down the stairs to get to work each morning.

Tony's grandparents worked in the hardware store, too. They lived in a house several blocks away from the store. They would drive about five minutes through side streets to get to work. This was not the case for Tony's mom. Tony's dad wanted to live in a more country-like setting, so his parents bought a small farm far outside the town. They bought their farmhouse quite a few years before Tony was born. He couldn't imagine living anywhere else. For years, Tony's mom drove to and from the hardware store with very little trouble. It took about 20 minutes for her to make the drive.

Five years ago, however, everything changed. Two large businesses were invited to town. These businesses promised to provide more than 3,000 jobs. They kept that promise, and then some. Now the town is bustling with thousands of cars on the roads, and new houses are going up everywhere, even near Tony's family's farm. Everyone in the town, including Tony's family, agrees that the new businesses are good for the town. The stores are flourishing. There are plenty of kids to fill ball teams and the local youth clubs, and Tony's class is bursting with more than 80 students. Tony can't even count all of his friends.

However, there is a downside. Roads in the area have become congested. Tony's mom drives on the same roads she has used for 20 years, but the drive that once took only 20 minutes now takes 40 minutes, at least. The townspeople are desperate for a new highway to go around the town.

No private company would be willing to build a highway because it wouldn't be profitable to do so. How could a company charge each driver entering the road? It would be necessary to set up tollbooths and allow very limited access to the road, and this just wouldn't be practical. Also, state legislators probably would not allow it. Tony's mom and other drivers bothered by congestion could go door to door, asking residents to contribute voluntarily to a fund for the construction of a new road. But they don't think that plan would work, either. Some people wouldn't consider the road important, so they wouldn't contribute. That would leave the cost to be paid by those who wanted the road.

Questions

1. Would private funding of the road be possible, considering that many people could use the road even if they did not contribute?

____

____

2. How will the townspeople get this badly needed road?

____

____

3. How does your community get new roads constructed?

____

____

NAME: ____________________ CLASS PERIOD: __________

Where Did the Money Go?

Study the paycheck stub to answer the questions that follow:

Employee Name:	John Taxpayer
Employee Social Security Number:	123-45-6789
Pay period ending:	12-31-10
Total wages	**$3,365.75**
Federal Tax Withheld (based on exemptions claimed on Form W-4)	**$310.45**
State Taxes	**$158.20**
Local Taxes	**$80.00**
Social Security Tax and Medicare Tax Withheld (FICA)	**$257.48**
Total deductions from paycheck	**$806.13**
Net Pay (the amount of your paycheck)	**$2,559.62**

1. What do you report on a Form W-4?

____

2. For what purposes are state taxes collected?

____

3. For what purposes are federal taxes collected?

____

4. Are FICA and federal income tax used to pay for the same things? Explain.

____

____

____

THEME 4

Introduction

Saving

If you could have a wish list, what would it include? An mp3 player? A new wardrobe? A computer? All of the above?

Wouldn't it be great to have all the money you needed right now to buy all the things you want? Chances are, though, you can't afford all the things on your wish list. That's why you have to make choices. One choice might be simply to do without one of the items, perhaps the mp3 player. Another choice, though, could be to save part of your income for a period of time until you have enough to pay for the mp3 player.

This might take a few weeks or months, or maybe even a year, but by choosing to give up spending now in order to save for the future, you would be able to buy that mp3 player eventually.

Why Save?

Introduction

In order to be successful at saving money, so that they can buy the things they want most, people usually set goals. Those who stick with their goals find satisfaction in two ways. They get more of the goods and services they want most. They also feel a lot of self-satisfaction and a sense of accomplishment—like the feeling a sprinter gets from winning a big race, or like a student who gets an A on a difficult test.

This lesson introduces you to the importance of setting goals for saving money and investing for the future. Some goals may be achieved quickly; others will take longer. The good news is: if you consider your options carefully, you'll probably make the right decisions, decisions that can help you reach the goals you have set.

No matter how little or how much money you want to save, you'll have to give up buying something now in order to save and invest for the future. The thing you give up is your opportunity cost.

If you save your loose change until you have a dollar to buy a large candy bar, you might be giving up the opportunity to buy gum from the gumball machine now and then. In that case, the gumballs are your opportunity cost. If you save $30 a month for six months until you have $180 for a concert ticket, you might give up the chance to spend money at an amusement park one month, download a few albums the next month, or treat your brother to a pizza the third month. In every case, the best spending alternative you give up when you decide to save is your opportunity cost.

You may find it difficult to imagine saving for five or six years to buy something you really want. That's a long time when you're 12 or 13. In fact, it's nearly half your life! But lots of people set long-term goals for themselves. They plan for things that are three, five, or even ten years in the future.

Vocabulary

Investing: Saving money in order to earn a financial return.

Long-term goals: Goals you plan to achieve in more than three years.

Medium-term goals: Goals you plan to achieve in two months to three years.

Opportunity cost: The next-best alternative that is given up when a choice is made.

Saving: The act of putting something aside for later use.

Scarcity: The economic problem that exists because of unlimited wants and limited resources.

Short-term goals: Goals you plan to achieve in fewer than two months.

NAME: ______________________ CLASS PERIOD: __________

How to Reach a Goal

Read the stories below and calculate whether the students at Elm Valley Middle School can reach their goals. Determine whether the goals are short-term (up to two months), medium-term (two months to three years), or long-term (more than three years). For any student who cannot reach his or her goal under the circumstances described, suggest ways in which the student might change the circumstances and reach his or her goal.

1. José tutors some sixth graders in math; for this work he earns $43 a week. He always puts $18 in his college fund, and he uses the rest for everyday expenses. At a jewelry store downtown, he spotted a bracelet that he'd like to buy for his mother's 40th birthday, two years from now. It is a real beauty, but the price is $250.

- If José puts aside $18 a week for college and spends $15 a week on everyday expenses, how long will it take him to save enough to buy the bracelet? (Do not consider any interest he might be earning on his savings.)
- Will it be a short-, medium- or long-term savings goal? Explain your answer.
- If Jose cannot save enough according to his present savings and spending plan, suggest some ways he might change his plan in order to reach his goal.

____

____

2. Lauren earns $20 every Saturday baby-sitting for her neighbors. She also receives an allowance of $12 per week for the chores she regularly does at home. Her parents have a rule that she must put half of her allowance in her college fund, a savings account from which she never withdraws any money.

Lauren plays tenor saxophone in the school band and has been renting an instrument from the music department. Last week Lauren saw a used sax at a music store in the mall. She'd really like to buy it, but it costs $210. Her parents told her that if she saves the $210, they'd pay the sales tax for her.

- If Lauren continues to contribute to her college fund, and saves every penny she earns, including her allowance, how long will it take her to save enough to buy the sax?
- Will it be a short-, medium-, or long-term savings goal? Explain your answer.
- If Lauren cannot save enough according to her present savings and spending plan, suggest ways she might change her plan in order to reach her goal.

____

____

3. Darnell works in his father's office on Mondays, Wednesdays, and Fridays; he earns $90 a week. He saves $24 each week in his college fund, gives $5 a week to charity, and spends $10 a week on snacks and entertainment.

Recently Darnell became interested in golf, and he wants to become a better player. Golf lessons at a local park cost $360 and begin in six weeks. Darnell wants to take these lessons.

- Is this a short-, medium-, or long-term savings goal?
- If Darnell continues his present saving, spending and sharing habits, will he be able to save enough money in time to attend the first golf lesson? Explain your answer.
- If Darnell will not be able to reach his goal by holding to his present plan for saving, spending, and sharing, how might he change his present plan in order to reach his savings goal?

____

____

NAME: ______________________________ CLASS PERIOD: __________

Rolling for a Goal:
A Game for Two or More Players

This game involves setting a savings goal and trying to reach it. Two or more people can play the game. Before starting the game, the teacher will provide the game cards. Shuffle them and place them in a pile. You will need two dice, a pencil, paper, and the score sheet (on the next page). Choose a person to go first.

1. Draw a card from the pile. This is your savings goal. Write this amount on line A of the Score Sheet.

2. Throw one die and multiply the number on the die by $10. Write this amount as the amount you can save each month on line B.

3. Calculate how many months you'll have to save in order to reach your goal, and write the answer on line C. (line A ÷ line B)

4. Identify the goal as either short-term (S), medium-term (M), or long-term (L), and write the appropriate letter on line D.

5. Roll two dice and multiply the two numbers to determine the number of months during which you will be able to save. Enter that number on line E.

6. Will you be able to reach your goal? Compare the number on line E with the one on line C. If E is greater than or equal to C, give yourself 2 points on line F; if not, give yourself 0 points on line F.

7. Play four rounds. Add the numbers in line F. The person with the most points wins. If winning scores are tied, those players can play additional rounds until there is one winner.

Scoring Sheet for Rolling for a Goal

	Round 1	Round 2	Round 3	Round 4
A Savings goal				
B Amount saved each month ($10 x roll of one die).				
C Number of months needed to meet goal (A÷B).				
D Short - (S), Medium - (M), or Long-term goal (L).				
E Number of months you will be able to save. (Roll of two dice multiplied together).				
F Yes, I will be able to meet my saving goal. (Give yourself 2 points.) No, I will not be able to meet my saving goal (0 points).				
Totals				

NAME: ______________________ CLASS PERIOD: __________

Short-, Medium-, and Long-Term Goals

The chart below shows how much money six people want to save. Each person is able to save a different amount each month. Calculate how long each person must save to reach his/her goal. Then write S, M, or L to indicate whether it is a short-, medium-, or long-term goal.

Person	Amount to be saved	Amount saved each month	How many months	How many years	Short-, medium-, or long-term
Abby	$780.00	$20.00			
Ben	25.00	15.00			
Cherise	700.00	35.00			
Danuka	800.00	70.00			
Emilio	90.00	50.00			
Festis	2,900.00	75.00			

Complete the following exercise about Cherise, based on your calculations in the above grid.

Cherise saves $35 every month. It will take her _______ months to reach her savings goal of $700. During those months, she could be spending her money, but instead she sticks to her savings plan. That means that every month she gives up some goods or services that she could have bought with the $35 she is saving.

In the blanks below, list the opportunity costs Cherise might incur during the months she saves toward her goal. (Be creative. Think of opportunity costs that could be associated with the months. For example, in April her opportunity cost might be a new raincoat for April showers.)

Month	Opportunity Cost	Explanation
January	______________	______________________________
February	______________	______________________________
March	______________	______________________________
April	______________	______________________________
May	______________	______________________________
June	______________	______________________________
July	______________	______________________________
August	______________	______________________________
September	______________	______________________________
October	______________	______________________________
November	______________	______________________________
December	______________	______________________________

Let Lenders and Borrowers Be

Introduction

Buying a gallon of milk is a pretty straightforward exchange. You walk into a store, grab a plastic jug, pay the cashier, and you're on your way. Saving, borrowing—and even investing—are a bit like buying products at a grocery store.

A bank, credit union, or other financial institution can be thought of as a supermarket. It brings a number of products together in one place so that buyers don't have to shop all over town for what they want. At a financial institution, consumers can cash a check, deposit money, apply for a loan, purchase a certificate of deposit, or get investment advice.

One of the most important roles of a financial institution is to act as an intermediary. Intermediaries bring together those who are in need of funds and those who wish to invest. For example, when a new company is just getting off the ground, it needs funding—for materials, equipment and supplies, maybe even to hire more workers.

Somewhere out there, investors are looking for an opportunity to earn a return on their funds. Often it is through a financial institution that the start-up company (that has a business opportunity) and the investor are brought together. The company finds its funder, and the investor finds an opportunity.

In this lesson, you will learn how banks, credit unions, savings and loan associations, and other financial institutions act as intermediaries, bringing together savers, borrowers, and investors. This information will give you food for thought as you begin to make investment decisions on your own.

Vocabulary

Financial intermediary: Banks, credit unions, pension funds, insurance companies, mutual funds and other financial institutions acting to bring together savers and borrowers as well as buyers and sellers of stock.

Interest: The price paid for using someone else's money.

Opportunity cost: The next-best alternative that is given up when a choice is made.

Demand: The quantity of a good or service that customers are willing and able to buy at all possible prices during a period of time.

Profit: The money a business has left over after selling its goods and services and paying its costs of production.

Revenue: The money a business receives from customers who buy its goods and services.

Supply: The quantity of a good or service that producers are willing and able to offer for sale at all possible prices during a period of time.

NAME: ______________________ CLASS PERIOD: __________

Calamity in Cow Town

Directions: Read the story below and answer the questions that follow.

Every town has at least one grocery store. In Cow Town, there are three large supermarkets. For the most part, all three markets get their groceries from the same food wholesalers and pay similar prices for the items they sell. This includes the milk that each market sells.

In the summer of 2010, Mrs. Jones created a new drink to serve her bridge club. She mixed milk, bananas, and pineapple juice together and called it banana milk. The ladies in the club couldn't get enough of the banana milk; the eight of them went through five gallons of milk, six pounds of bananas, and two gallons of pineapple juice that day. They each asked for the recipe and, on the way home from Mrs. Jones's house, they each bought two gallons of milk, along with the other ingredients.

The next day each lady made up a batch of banana milk and served it to her children, grandchildren, the neighbors, and anyone else who happened by. Everyone loved the stuff and headed for the grocery stores to get milk. Day after day, more people came to know and love banana milk; day after day, people bought more milk than they ever had bought before.

The grocers in Cow Town would place the usual amount of milk on the shelves in the morning, and it would be gone by mid-afternoon. Then it was gone by noon. Then it was gone by mid-morning. Finally, the grocers were simply handing the milk to the awaiting hordes early in the morning. The grocers tried to get more milk, but there were only so many cows in Cow Town.

What could the grocers do to reduce the frenzy? There was only one answer. The grocers raised the price of milk. First, they raised their prices by ten cents a gallon. Then 20 cents. Then 30 cents. As they raised the price, they sold fewer and fewer gallons until, one day, the milk actually stayed on the shelf the whole day before the last gallon was grabbed.

Yes, in the summer of 2010, the people of Cow Town learned a lesson in supply and demand. What happened to the people of Cow Town who cut their milk consumption because of the higher price? They drank orange juice instead.

Questions

1. What happened to the demand for milk in the story? Why?

2. What happened to the supply of milk in the story? Why?

3. What happened to the price of milk in the story? Why?

4. What do you think happened to the prices of bananas and pineapple juice?

5. If you were one of the dairy farmers in Cow Town and the price of milk went up, what changes might you have made on your farm?

NAME: ______________________________ CLASS PERIOD: ____________

Financial Terms

Match the terms (numbers) with their descriptions (letters).

1. The next-best alternative given up when a decision is made	A. saver
2. The difference between revenue and costs	B. profit
3. Banks are sometimes called this	C. opportunity cost
4. The supplier of funds for loans	D. interest
5. The demander of loans	E. borrower
6. The price of money	F. financial intermediary

LESSON 12

Types of Savings Plans and Investments

Introduction

If you saved $100 under your mattress, in 50 years you'd still have $100, right?

Well, yes and no. Even though you would still have $100 in your hand, you couldn't buy as much with your $100 now as you could have bought 50 years ago, because things tend to get more expensive over time. After all, back in the 1950s you could see a movie for a quarter, and the price of a phone call was only five cents. Now things cost more. That's called inflation: a general increase in the prices of goods and services. In order to "keep up with inflation," people don't save their money under a mattress. They have a number of different options when it comes to saving and investing. One option is to put their money in a bank or some other financial institution.

Most financial institutions offer a number of ways to save and earn interest. In this lesson, you will learn about some of them: regular savings accounts, money market deposit accounts, and certificates of deposit (CDs). All these savings plans are safe and pay interest. The extent to which these plans are convertible to cash depends on the type of instrument. A different type of savings instrument, a U.S. Savings Bond, also has important advantages and disadvantages for savers. It's important to understand all the pros and cons when you choose where to save your money.

Vocabulary

Certificate of deposit (CD): An account where your deposit remains for a set period of time, called a term (e.g., 6 months, 1 year, 5 years, etc.). These accounts may be insured and usually earn higher rates of interest than a regular savings account. CDs with longer terms earn higher rates of interest. There is a penalty for withdrawing funds before the end of the term.

Financial risk: The risk of losing principal (the amount of money invested), and the return on the principal.

Inflation: A general increase in the prices of goods and services.

Inflation risk: The risk that the value of investments will not increase at least as rapidly as the rate of inflation.

Interest rate risk: The risk that interest rates may change while the saver is "locked in" to a specific interest rate on a time deposit.

Money market deposit account: An interest-bearing account that offers limited check-writing privileges. These accounts may require a minimum balance and may have other limitations. The interest paid on money market deposit accounts may be higher or lower than statement savings accounts. Deposits can be added to at any time, but withdrawals may be limited (without incurring a fee or penalty).

Opportunity cost: The next-best alternative that is given up when a choice is made.

Portfolio: A person's or institution's collection of savings and investments.

Savings instrument: Arrangements by means of which people save money, including savings accounts, certificates of deposit (CDs), money market deposit accounts, and U.S. Savings Bonds.

Savings account: An interest-bearing account that can be opened with a small amount of money; funds can easily be deposited or withdrawn.

United States Savings Bond: Technically, a loan to the U.S. government upon which you earn interest. There are two major types of U.S. Savings Bonds. Series EE are purchased for less than their face value, then redeemed at their full value when they mature; for example, a $100 bond costs $50. $100 is paid to the owner when the bond matures. Series EE bonds issued on or after May 1, 2005, earn a fixed rate of return. Another kind (Series I) is sold at its face value (you pay $100 for a $100 bond) and earns variable interest over the time it is held. The interest rate on these bonds is designed to keep pace with inflation. Series I bonds pay off only when redeemed. There is an interest penalty if you cash them in before five years.

NAME: ______________________________ CLASS PERIOD: __________

Types of Guaranteed Savings Instruments

Most of the savings methods described here are guaranteed in most commercial banks, savings and loan associations, savings banks, and credit unions. The guarantee means depositors will not lose the money they have deposited. The U.S. federal government guarantees an individual's deposits up to $250,000 per banking institution through the Federal Deposit Insurance Corporation (FDIC). The National Credit Union Association (NCUA) has the same type of insurance for credit unions. U.S. Savings Bonds are not guaranteed by any insurance; bonds are debts of the U.S. Treasury. The federal government, though, stands behind the payment of these debts, so they are quite safe.

Savings Accounts

Savings accounts have traditionally provided a way to save money in a bank. As long as you keep money in your savings account, the bank pays you interest and your money grows. The most common kind of savings account is a statement savings account. For this account, the bank sends you a statement that details all of your deposits and withdrawals and the interest you've earned, either once a month or once a quarter (every three months). Interest rates for these accounts are usually lower than rates for other types of savings instruments, but you can open a savings account with very little money. You can also withdraw your money whenever you like.

Savings Account Advantages

- Your money is easy to access; you do not have to leave it in the bank for a specific amount of time. You can withdraw it without any penalty.
- The interest rate paid on the deposit can increase as general interest rates increase.
- You can open the account with a small amount of money.

Savings Account Disadvantages

- Traditional savings accounts pay lower interest rates than other saving plans.
- Interest rates can go down as general interest rates go down.
- The bank may charge a service fee if the account balance falls below a certain minimum.

Certificate of Deposit Accounts (CDs)

Certificate of deposit accounts, also known as CDs, are accounts in which people deposit a specific amount of money for a specific time period. For example, a depositor might put $500 into a CD for six months or one year. Generally, the longer the time agreed to, the higher the interest rate. A penalty is charged for early withdrawals from CDs.

Most CDs guarantee ("lock in") a rate of interest for the life of the CD, but some offer rates that may be adjusted up and down. "Bump up" CDs allow depositors to increase the interest rate to a higher rate one time if rates are going up. They also allow depositors to add to the initial deposit.

CD Advantages

- Banks generally pay higher interest rates on CDs than on traditional savings accounts. Bankers know depositors probably will not withdraw their money until the agreed-upon time because of the penalty (lost interest) that is imposed for early withdrawals.
- The locked-in interest rate can be advantageous if general interest rates go down during the time period of the CD.

CD Disadvantages

- Depositors pay a substantial penalty if they withdraw their money early.
- The locked-in interest rate can be disadvantageous if interest rates increase during the time period of the CD.
- Generally, a minimum deposit, such as $500, is required to open a CD account.

Money Market Deposit Accounts

Money market deposit accounts are similar to checking accounts, because depositors can write checks on money market deposit accounts. They are insured through the Federal Deposit Insurance Corporation, a government agency.

Do not confuse money market deposit accounts with money market mutual funds. Money market mutual funds are offered by financial institutions other than banks and are not insured by the FDIC. Many of these are offered by mutual funds and brokerage firms.

An increasing number of money market deposit accounts may be combined with statement checking accounts. The interest paid on these accounts may be less than the interest paid on statement savings accounts, especially when there is no limitation on the number of checks written. In other cases, the interest rate may be higher than the rate for statement savings accounts. Rates vary from one financial institution to another.

Money Market Deposit Account Advantages

- Money market deposit accounts allow periodic withdrawals, just like traditional savings accounts, with no penalty. It is very convenient to be able to write a check to withdraw money from this kind of savings account.
- Interest paid on savings increases as general interest rates increase.
- Money market deposit accounts may pay a higher rate of interest than regular checking accounts.

Money Market Deposit Account Disadvantages

- Money market accounts require a significant minimum balance, often $1,000 or higher.
- The number of checks depositors can write without extra charges may be very small.
- The interest rate goes down as general interest rates go down.
- The interest rate may be lower than the rate on a savings account.

United States Savings Bonds

Savings bonds are debt instruments issued by the U.S. Government. The person who buys the bond is the lender and the government is the borrower. Some savings bonds (Series EE) are purchased for one-half their face value and are later cashed at face value. Others (Series I) are purchased at face value. Series I bonds have a variable interest rate to help keep up with inflation.

U.S. Savings Bond Advantages

- Savings bonds can be purchased for as little as $25 (a $50 Series EE bond).
- Savings bonds generally pay a higher rate of interest than a savings account.
- Series EE interest rates remain the same on existing bonds when general interest rates decrease.
- Savers may not have to pay state and local income taxes on interest earned on government savings bonds.
- Parents who use savings bonds for their child's college education also enjoy a tax advantage.
- Bonds are less risky than other long-term investments such as stocks.

U.S. Savings Bond Disadvantages

- Bonds usually earn less than other long-term investments such as stocks.
- There is a penalty of three months' interest if a Series I bond is sold before five years.
- Interest rates of Series I bonds can go down if general interest rates go down.
- Owners of savings bonds lose access to funds until the bonds can be cashed out.
- Series EE bonds issued on or after May 1, 2005, earn a fixed return, so the interest rate will not go up if general interest rates rise.

After you have read the above information about savings instruments, decide where you should put your savings in the following situations:

1. You have savings of $100 that you may need within two months.

____

2. You have savings of $1,000 that you may need within three years.

____

3. You have savings of $1,000 that you may need within three months.

____

4. You have savings of $10,000, but you wish to make periodic withdrawals.

____

5. You have savings of $1,000 that you will need in three years. You believe the interest rate will be decreasing in the next couple of years.

____

6. A couple receives $2,000 from family members on the birth of their baby. The parents want to put this money toward their newborn's college education.

____

NAME: ____________________ CLASS PERIOD: __________

Savings Plans in My Community

Savings instruments	Minimum balance or deposit	Interest rate	Penalty for withdrawal	Fees
Statement savings account				
6-month CD				
12-month CD				
24-month CD				
Money market deposit account				

Name of bank or institution: ____________________

____

Where did you get this information? (For example, an interview of a bank representative, from the Internet, or from a newspaper.)

____

____

____

Are any of the accounts insured? If so, by whom, and up to what amount?

____

____

____

NAME: ______________________ CLASS PERIOD: __________

Now or Later?

One year ago you placed $975 in a savings account that paid interest at a rate of three percent. You were saving to buy one of the items listed below. The items changed in price over the year. Look at the current prices for the items. You will see that in some cases it was good that you waited. In other cases, you are worse off. Calculate the percentage change in price to discover just how much better or worse off you are. Give it a try!

Item	Last year's price	This year's price	% change
Computer	$997.00	$897.30	
Digital camcorder	$1,005.00	$954.75	
Plasma flat-panel TV	$3,000.00	$2,070.00	
Car stereo system	$995.00	$1,074.60	
One year's wardrobe	$995.00	$1,094.50	

Amount in your savings account at the end of the year: ______________
(Principal plus interest)

1. Which items could you purchase with your savings if you were to buy them in the present year?

____

2. Which items would you have been able to purchase with your savings last year?

____

3. Which item had the greatest percentage increase in price?

____

4. Which item had the greatest percentage decrease in price?

____

5. For which items did you lose buying power over the year?

____

NAME: ______________________ CLASS PERIOD: __________

Decisions, Decisions

Choosing the right savings plan or investment method can be difficult. You have just discussed the risks that go along with various choices. Apply your knowledge of interest rate risk and inflation risk to determine which savings methods you would choose in the following situations. Be sure to explain why the method you choose is the best for the situation. Choose from a statement savings account, a U.S. Savings Bond, a money market deposit account, or a certificate of deposit (CD).

a. You have savings of $100 that you need within two months, and you think interest rates will be going down in the next few years.

Savings method ______________ Why? ______________________________

b. You have $1,000 in savings that you may need within three years, and you believe interest rates will be rising over that time.

Savings method ______________ Why? ______________________________

c. You have $1,000 in savings that you may need within the next three years, and you believe interest rates will be declining.

Savings method ______________ Why? ______________________________

d. You have $50 that you want to put away for your college costs in seven years. You believe interest rates will be increasing for most of those seven years.

Savings method ______________ Why? ______________________________

e. You have savings of $10,000 from which you need to make periodic withdrawals. You believe interest rates will be decreasing in the next few years.

Savings method ______________ Why? ______________________________

NAME: ______________________ CLASS PERIOD: __________

Part 1: Types of Savings Plans

Match the best savings plan with the situation.

Options:

A Savings account

B Certificate of deposit

C Money market deposit account

D U.S. Savings Bond

Situations:

1. Alfredo has $100 and wants to be able to withdraw it at any time without penalty.

2. Willie is eight years old and wants to save the $25 he received for his birthday for college.

3. Juanita will soon begin attending college. She just inherited $5,000 from Aunt Mildred. She will need it for college expenses beginning in two months.

4. Garth has $10,000 in savings that he will not need for a while. He believes interest rates will be going down in the next year.

5. Kari has $2,000 in savings. She wants to earn the most interest possible before she needs it for college in five years. She believes that interest rates will increase in the next few years.

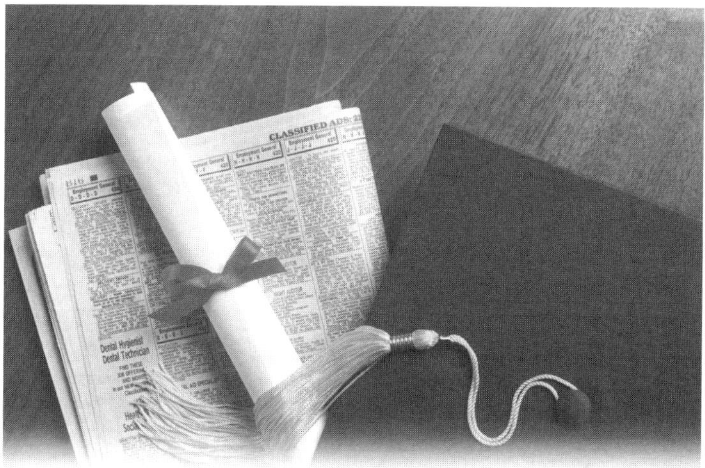

NAME: ______________________ CLASS PERIOD: __________

Part 2: Weighing All the Risks

In this lesson, you have learned about three types of risks. For each of the following savings plan options and investments, identify the major risk. After naming the risk, give reasons for your response.

The Risks:

A Inflation risk

B Interest rate risk

C Financial risk

The Options:

1. Savings account: ______________________

____

____

2. Certificate of Deposit: ______________________

____

____

3. U.S. Savings Bond: ______________________

____

____

Who Pays and Who Receives?

Introduction

A wise person once said, "You can work for your money, or you can let your money work for you." You work for your money when you get a job and begin to earn regular paychecks. Your money works for you when you save and invest it wisely.

Saving is a good idea because the money you save earns interest. Did you ever stop to think about how much interest you can earn on your savings?

In this lesson you will learn about saving, and about the effects of simple and compound interest. You'll use a quick formula, called the Rule of 72, to calculate how long it takes to double your money. Finally, you will find out that three things affect how hard your money can work for you:

- the amount you save,
- the rate of interest,
- the length of time you leave money in an account.

As strange as it may seem, banks are businesses—just as grocery stores, gas stations, and theaters are businesses. Every business wants to please its customers and earn a profit. Without a profit, a company will lose money and have to shut down.

Banks earn profits by lending money to borrowers. The borrowers have to pay a price for the loan; that price is called interest.

Where do banks get the money they lend to borrowers? That's where you come in. Based in part on the amount of deposits you and others make, banks earn money by making loans of this money to borrowers. These loans are used by people to buy cars and houses, and by businesses to buy machines and buildings. The bank is paid interest by its borrowers, and in turn, the bank pays you interest for using your deposited money.

In order to make a profit, the bank charges more interest to borrowers than it pays to savers. For example, borrowers might pay 8 percent interest, and savers might earn 5 percent interest. The difference is the bank's markup. The bank uses its markup to pay its employees, buy computers, and pay other expenses of the firm. The bank's return for taking a risk—its profit—is also part of the markup. Banking, like other enterprises, can be a risky business; after all, customers might default on a loan, which means the customer does not repay the loan. An understanding of banks and interest is important; it can help you make wise saving and investing decisions now and in the future.

Vocabulary

Compound interest: Interest computed on the sum of the principal and previously earned interest.

Compounding: The practice of leaving interest earned "on deposit" so that it too earns interest.

Interest: The price paid for using someone else's money.

Interest rate: The price paid for using someone else's money, expressed as a percentage.

Principal: The amount deposited in savings without including interest earned.

Rule of 72: A formula that can be used to calculate how long it takes for invested money to double.

Simple interest: Interest earned on the principal and paid out to a depositor.

NAME: ______________________ CLASS PERIOD: ___________

Simple Interest

The Simple Interest Group will use this form. Your teacher will show you how to complete the form.

A	B	C	D	E	F	G
Deposit Cycle	Beginning Balance (G) from previous line	Deposited Amount	New Balance (B) + (C)	Rate of Interest	Interest earned and paid out (D) x (E)	Ending Balance (Same as D)
1	0	10	10	20%	2	10
2		10		20%		
3		10		20%		
4		10		20%		
5		10		20%		
6		10		20%		
Total						

NAME: ____________________ CLASS PERIOD: __________

Compound Interest

The Compound Interest Group will use this form. Your teacher will show you how to complete the form.

Round decimals to the next-highest whole number.

A	B	C	D	E	F	G
Deposit Cycle	Beginning Balance (G) from previous line	Deposited Amount	New Balance (B) + (C)	Rate of Interest	Interest earned and left in account (D) x (E)	Ending Balance (D) + (F)
1	0	10	10	20%	2	12
2		10		20%		
3		10		20%		
4		10		20%		
5		10		20%		
6		10		20%		
Total						

NAME: ______________________ CLASS PERIOD: __________

Simple Interest: When and Why Would People Choose It?

Ms. Wirtz is a former magazine editor who retired at the age of 55. She has $60,000 in an account that earns 6 percent interest annually. Because she needs the interest for some of her living expenses, Ms. Wirtz has arranged to receive an interest check from the bank every quarter (four times a year). In this way, she has money to live on, and her $60,000 principal doesn't decrease. What is the amount Ms. Wirtz receives every quarter? The formula below shows how to calculate her simple interest and quarterly interest payments (note that the annual interest rate is expressed as a decimal).

Principal x annual interest rate x time = simple interest ÷ 4 = quarterly payment

Ms. Wirtz' annual interest and quarterly payment are shown in the first line of the grid on this page. Use the formula to calculate simple interest, interest rate, principal, and quarterly payments in the rest of the grid, and fill in the blank spaces.

Principal	x	Interest Rate	x	Time	=	Simple Interest	÷ 4 =	Quarterly Payment
$60,000	x	6%	x	1 year	=	$3,600	÷ 4 =	$900
$20,000	x	5%	x	1 year	=		÷ 4 =	
	x	10%	x	1 year	=	$1,000	÷ 4 =	
$80,000	x		x	1 year	=	$5,600	÷ 4 =	
$75,000	x	9%	x	1 year	=		÷ 4 =	
$125,000	x	8%	x	1 year	=		÷ 4 =	
$200,000	x		x	1 year	=	$14,000	÷ 4 =	
$40,000	x		x	1 year	=		÷ 4 =	$500
	x	4%	x	1 year	=		÷ 4 =	$1,000
$100,000	x		x	1 year	=		÷ 4 =	$2,500

NOTE: People who hold certain interest-earning accounts, such as certificates of deposit, can have payments sent to them quarterly. That way they can use their interest for daily living expenses, travel, or other purchases. Even though they spend the interest, they maintain the principal.

EXERCISE
13.3

NAME: ______________________ CLASS PERIOD: __________

Racing Toward a Goal

Eight members of the Slug Hill Stock Car Team have challenged each other to begin a savings plan. They know that by making annual deposits and not withdrawing any money, their interest will compound and they will reach their goals. They also know that three things affect how their savings will grow:

- How much they deposit
- What the interest rate is
- How long the money remains on deposit

Even though they will all reach their goal, they will not do so at the same time. Select one of the drivers on the next page and, using the calculation sheet on page 100, calculate how long it will take the driver to reach the goal. Complete the table and fill in the blanks in the box at the bottom of page 100.

Compare your results with those of other team (class) members to determine the order in which the drivers reach the finish line. Enter the overall results in the list below.

1st Place ______________________

2nd Place ______________________

3rd Place ______________________

4th Place ______________________

5th Place ______________________

6th Place ______________________

7th Place ______________________

8th Place ______________________

Driver A

Annual Deposit = $2,000
Interest Rate = 6%
Goal = $40,000

Driver B

Annual Deposit = $2,000
Interest Rate = 10%
Goal = $29,000

Driver C

Annual Deposit = $3,000
Interest Rate = 6%
Goal = $41,000

Driver D

Annual Deposit = $3,000
Interest Rate = 10%
Goal = $61,000

Driver E

Annual Deposit = $4,000
Interest Rate = 6%
Goal = $35,000

Driver F

Annual Deposit = $4,000
Interest Rate = 10%
Goal = $26,000

Driver G

Annual Deposit = $5,000
Interest Rate = 6%
Goal = $52,000

Driver H

Annual Deposit = $5,000
Interest Rate = 10%
Goal = $42,000

NAME: ______________________ CLASS PERIOD: __________

Calculation Sheet for Racing Toward a Goal

A	B	C	D	E	F	G
Year	Beginning Balance (column G of previous year)	Annual Deposit	New Balance (B) + (C)	Interest Rate	Interest Earned (D) x (E)	Ending Balance (D) + (F)
1	0					
2						
3						
4						
5						
6						
7						
8						
9						
10						
11						
12						
13						
14						

Note: Round cents to the nearest whole number.

Driver __________ wants to save $ ______________
(insert letter)

It will take ______________ years to achieve the goal.

NAME: ______________________ CLASS PERIOD: __________

Checking Out the Rule of 72: Does It Work?

The Rule of 72 provides a way of estimating how long it takes for money to double. Test the Rule of 72 by completing the following exercise.

The formula for the Rule of 72 is to divide 72 by the interest rate (expressed in percentage terms). This gives you the approximate number of years it takes to double an investment earning at that interest rate.

72 ÷ interest rate = number of years until money doubles

How would this formula work? Begin with $100,000. With a partner and an on-line calculator, figure out how long it takes for this $100,000 to become $200,000 at these interest rates: 2%, 3%, 4%, 6%, 8%, 9% and 12%.

Use this website, or a similar one: http://www.1728.com/compint.htm

Follow these procedures when using the online calculator:

Solve for YEARS

Input *principal* (do not use commas): 100000

Input *total* (do not use commas): 200000 (double the principal)

Input *interest rate* (do NOT use decimals): 2 or 3 or 4 and so on

Click on CALCULATE

You will get an answer in years.

Does the number of years multiplied by the interest rate equal about 72?

Complete this form, using the calculator on the web site.

A	B	C	D	E
Principal	Double the Principal	Interest Rate Percentage	No. of years for money to double (from Web Calculator)	Does Column C x Column D = approximately 72?
$100,000	$200,000	2		
$100,000	$200,000	3		
$100,000	$200,000	4		
$100,000	$200,000	6		
$100,000	$200,000	8		
$100,000	$200,000	9		
$100,000	$200,000	12		

NAME: ______________________ CLASS PERIOD: __________

Factors That Affect How Money Grows

Three factors affect how money grows in an account:

- Amount of deposit,
- Interest rate,
- Length of time the money remains on deposit.

Demonstrate these three factors by completing the grid. When you finish, make a generalization about the three factors that affect how money grows.

Beginning values:
Amount $5,000
Interest rate 5%
Time 5 years

Change only the amount:
Amount $10,000
Interest rate 5%
Time 5 years

Change only the interest rate:
Amount $5,000
Interest rate 10%
Time 5 years

Change only the time:
Amount $5,000
Interest rate 10%
Time 10 years

Year	Year Start Balance	Interest Rate	Interest Earned	Year End Balance
1	$5,000	5%		
2		5%		
3		5%		
4		5%		
5		5%		
1	$10,000	5%		
2		5%		
3		5%		
4		5%		
5		5%		
1	$5,000	10%		
2		10%		
3		10%		
4		10%		
5		10%		
1	$5,000	5%		
2		5%		
3		5%		
4		5%		
5		5%		
6		5%		
7		5%		
8		5%		
9		5%		
10		5%		

Stocks and Mutual Funds

Introduction

One characteristic of a market economy is private ownership of property. Property is not just land and real estate; it is anything of economic value that belongs to you. Your stereo is your property, a baseball card collection is your property, and shares of stock in a corporation are property, too. If you own shares of stock, you have equity in the corporation. Equity means ownership.

By owning stock in a corporation, you become part-owner of that company. You can earn dividends, which are distributed from profits of the company. You can also earn a capital gain when you sell shares of stock at a higher price than you paid for them. Your shares of stock are called equities.

Stocks are bought and sold in the stock market. There are actual physical stock markets such as the New York Stock Exchange, and there are stock markets that operate on the Internet such as NASDAQ. When stockholders want to sell stock they own, they often contact a broker who acts as an agent for the seller by selling the stock for the stockholder. When someone wants to buy stock in a company, he or she often contacts a broker who acts as an agent for the buyer in purchasing the stock. The stock buyer pays for the stock, and the stock seller gets the money. The brokers get a small percentage of the money for the service they perform.

For the stock buyer, there is no guarantee that the investment will be successful. As an owner of stocks, you have some say about how the corporation should be run. You also get to share in the profits that are made. But there is no guarantee that the corporation in which you are an owner will be successful. If the corporation does not make a profit, there is no built-in safety net or insurance to reimburse you for your losses.

Then why do so many people—more than 50 percent of Americans—invest in the stock market? Many people choose to invest more of their money in the stock market rather than putting it into CDs, money market deposit accounts, statement savings accounts or U.S. Savings Bonds. People invest in the stock market because of the possibility of earning a better return.

Vocabulary

Capital gain: Gain from selling stocks or other investments for more than what was paid for them.

Capital loss: Loss from selling stocks or other investments for less than what was paid for them.

Dividend: Periodic payment distributed from profits of a corporation to its stockholders.

Equity: The value of property that is owned, including shares of stocks in a corporation.

Stock: A share of ownership in a company.

Stock market: Where shares of stocks are bought and sold (can be a specific, physical place or sales can take place online).

The Pie War

CAST OF CHARACTERS	
Pretty Pies, store owner	**Lydia,** customer
Perfect Pies, store owner	**Kendall,** person at the party
Meredith, customer	**Narrator**

Students will play the parts of pie-store owners, the customers (Meredith and Lydia), and Kendall. The teacher should serve as narrator.

Choose the two pie-store owners and have them stand next to each other at the front of the room.

Choose the two customers and have them stand at opposite ends of the front of the room.

Choose Kendall and have him or her stand toward the back of the room.

Begin the play.

Narrator: This is a story about two businesses: Pretty Pies and Perfect Pies. The owner of Pretty Pies has a little store where she makes pies in the back and sells them in the front. She makes the best pies. She uses fresh fruit for the filling. The crust is brown and flakey, and the pies never fall apart when sliced.

The owner of Perfect Pies also has a little store where he makes pies in the back and sells them in the front. He makes perfect pies. He uses fresh fruit for the filling. The crust is brown and flakey, and the pies never fall apart when sliced.

It just so happens that Pretty Pies and Perfect Pies are located right next door to each other, in identical buildings. They produce the same number of pies at the exact same cost. They sell the same number of pies at the exact same price, so their profits are exactly the same. These companies are identical in every way.

One day, Meredith is walking down the street and happens upon the Pretty Pies store.

Meredith: *(Walk down the street toward Pretty Pies store. Go up to Pretty Pies.)* Hello, I need a pie.

Pretty Pies owner: I have great pies. I know you will like them. See? *(Hold up pretend pie.)* They have a golden brown crust and are overloaded with fruit.

Meredith: This IS a great pie. I'll take it! By the way, how long have you been doing this?

Pretty Pies owner: About two years.

Meredith: Is it a good business?

Pretty Pies owner: The best!

Meredith: How good is it?

Pretty Pies owner: Last year, I made a lot of money. People come from all over to buy my pies.

Meredith: Do you own this store by yourself?

Pretty Pies owner: Yes, it's all mine. But, I wouldn't mind having an investor. If I had a little more money, I could do some things around here to make the store even better.

Meredith: I have $1,000 I would like to invest. I could give it to you; then, if you are profitable at the end of the year, you could give me a part of the profit.

Pretty Pies owner: Okay. You give me $1,000. *(Act like you're writing something down on paper.)* Let me give you this piece of paper called a stock. It says you own part of my business. If I make a profit, I'll share some with you.

Meredith: Great. See ya. *(Leave the store and go back to your original spot.)*

Narrator: Just as Meredith leaves the store, here comes Lydia down the street.

Lydia: *(Walk down the street toward Perfect Pies. Go up to Perfect Pies.)* Hi, I would like to buy a pie.

Perfect Pies owner: I have great pies. I know you will like them. See? *(Hold up pretend pie.)* They have a golden brown crust and are overloaded with fruit.

Lydia: This IS a great pie. I'll take it! By the way, how long have you been doing this?

Perfect Pies owner: About two years.

Lydia: Is it a good business?

Perfect Pies owner: The best!

Lydia: How good is it?

Perfect Pies owner: Last year, I made a lot of money. People come from all over to buy my pies.

Lydia: Do you own this store by yourself?

Perfect Pies owner: Yes, it's all mine. But, I wouldn't mind having an investor. If I had a little more money, I could do some things around here to make the store even better.

Lydia: I have $1,000 I would like to invest. I could give it to you; then, if you are profitable at the end of the year, you could give me a part of the profit.

Perfect Pies owner: Okay. You give me $1,000. *(Act like you're writing something down on paper.)* Let me give you this piece of paper called a stock. It says you own part of my business. If I make a profit, I'll share some with you.

Lydia: Great. See ya. *(Leave the store and go back to your original spot.)*

Narrator: A year passed, and both business owners made improvements to their businesses, using the $1,000 investment each had received. Once again, the two businesses received identical revenue, had identical costs, and earned identical profits. Each business owner scheduled a visit with his or her respective investor.

Meredith: *(Walk to Pretty Pies.)* Hi, how did things go this year?

Pretty Pies owner: We had great success. I appreciate your financial investment and your faith in my business. I would like to give you $500 as your part of the profit.

Meredith: Wow! I just made $500 for just a $1,000 investment. Do you realize that is a 50 percent return on my money?

Pretty Pies owner: Yes. You deserve it for wisely investing in my company.

Meredith: Thank you very much. I am glad to be a shareholder in your company. I'll be back next year to see how you're doing.

Pretty Pies owner: I'll be here. I hope to give you another 50 percent return! (Walk back to your original position.)

Narrator: Just as Meredith was leaving Pretty Pies, Lydia was arriving at Perfect Pies.

Lydia: (Walk to Perfect Pies.) Hi, how did things go this year?

Perfect Pies owner: We had great success. I appreciate your financial investment and your faith in my business. I could give you $500 as your part of the profit, but I would like to take a large part of my profit and your profit and buy a second crust-making machine and a fruit-slicing machine. If I had these machines I could double the number of pies I make. I would be producing twice as many pies each hour, so I could offer my pies at a lower price. People would buy their pies here instead of buying them from my competitor next door. Next year, we would have a much larger profit to share.

Lydia: That makes sense. Go ahead and do that. I'll be back next year to see how you're doing.

Perfect Pies owner: I'll be here. I hope to give you a 100 percent return! *(Walk back to your original position.)*

Narrator: A few months later, Meredith and Lydia ran into Kendall at a holiday party. They talked about the things that young adults talk about—their jobs, their apartments, and their cars. They also talked about how expensive it is to buy furniture, maintain their cars, and pay their bills. Finally, the subject turned to earning money.

Kendall: I work 40 hours each week, and I make $15.00 per hour. That's enough to pay my rent, buy food, maintain my car, and add small amounts of money to my savings account, but I don't have money left over to buy some of the fun things I would like to have. I would like to find a way to make money, but I don't want to work more hours. I guess there is no way to earn money without working more.

Meredith: Actually, you CAN earn money without working more hours. There was a bit of risk involved, but I did it by investing in a pie company.

Lydia: You invested in a pie company? What a coincidence. So did I! My pie company is doing great!

Meredith: So is mine.

Kendall: I would like to find an investment like yours.

Meredith: I might be interested in selling you my share of the pie company—for the right price.

Lydia: I might be interested in selling you MY share of the pie company—for the right price.

Kendall: I would like to invest in one of the pie companies. *(Turn to face Meredith.)* Should I invest in your company? *(Turn to face Lydia.)* Or should I invest in your company? *(Turn to face both Lydia and Meredith.)* Tell me about your companies.

Lydia: The company I invested in is doing very well.

Meredith: So is mine.

Lydia: Mine is highly profitable and will earn even greater profits next year.

Meredith: So will mine.

Kendall: I don't want to cause an argument. Just tell me this. How big a return have you received on your investment?

Lydia: I haven't received a return because my pie company used the money to buy two machines that will make more pies.

Meredith: I received a 50 percent return.

Kendall: Wow! A 50 percent return?

Narrator: *(Ask the class:)* Which pie company stock did Kendall buy? (Pretty Pies.) Which company do you think will have earned more money, compared to the last year? *(Perfect Pies.)* Let's see what happened.

Meredith: *(Walk to Pretty Pies.)* Hi, how did things go this year?

Pretty Pies owner: We did well. We earned almost as much profit as we did last year. Some people who used to buy pies from me began to buy their pies next door. They said those pies were just as good and they didn't cost as much.

Meredith: I'm sorry to hear that.

Pretty Pies owner: It's okay. I still earned a profit and I can share it with you. Here is $200.

Meredith: That's nice. A 20 percent return is very good. Of course, it's not as good as last year's 50 percent return. Maybe it will be better next year. See you then. Bye. *(Walk back to your position.)*

Narrator: Just as Meredith was leaving the store, Lydia was arriving at Perfect Pies store.

Lydia: *(Walk to Perfect Pies.)* Hi, how did things go this year?

Perfect Pies owner: We had great success. Just as I had hoped, I was able to make twice as many pies, so I was able to offer them at a lower price. I sold pies to many people who used to get their pies from the company next door. I earned a very large profit. Here is a check for $1,000. This is your share of the profit I earned.

Lydia: Wow! That's a 100 percent return this year. I've never heard of a return that high.

Perfect Pies owner: Well, we hope to be just as successful next year, too!

Narrator: Other investors began watching the two companies. They saw that Pretty Pies store was not likely to earn more profit in the future. However, they were impressed with the Perfect Pies store. The investors expected this store's profit to grow more and more each year. So, the investors asked if they could also buy shares of the Perfect Pies store.

THE END *(Bow and take your seats.)*

With a partner, answer the following questions:

A. Why did Perfect Pies become more profitable than Pretty Pies?

____

____

____

B. What will Pretty Pies have to do to compete with Perfect Pies?

____

____

____

NAME: ____________________ CLASS PERIOD: __________

Pie Potential

Pretty Pies and Perfect Pies began to sell stock. Research analysts from three brokerage firms began investigating the pie companies, looking for strong stocks for their customers. Unlike Kendall, they were unimpressed with the big dividend offered by Pretty Pies. On the other hand, they liked what they saw in the management of Perfect Pies. They appreciated Perfect Pies' focus on future growth as evidenced by the capital investment in the pie crust machine and the fruit slicing machine.

The research analysts urged their firms begin to recommend that their customers buy Perfect Pies stock. They weren't optimistic about the growth of Pretty Pies, however, and did not recommend Pretty Pies stock.

As the customers of the brokerage firms began to buy Perfect Pies, the stock price for Perfect Pies increased. This was like a signal to other potential stock buyers. As they saw the price of Perfect Pies stock increasing, they examined the information the researchers had analyzed and decided they also wanted stock in Perfect Pies. The stock price continued to go up.

As for Pretty Pies, the stock price never increased. The analysts who studied Pretty Pies assumed that the best-case outlook for Pretty Pies was that it would continue to make the same profit it had made before. The worst-case outlook was that it would not be able to compete with Perfect Pies and would go out of business.

Answer these questions:

A. Which company's stock did research analysts recommend?

____

B. What was it about the Perfect Pies operations that impressed the analysts?

____

C. What was the signal to other stock purchasers that Perfect Pies was a good investment?

____

D. What was the signal to other stock purchasers that Pretty Pies was not a good investment?

____

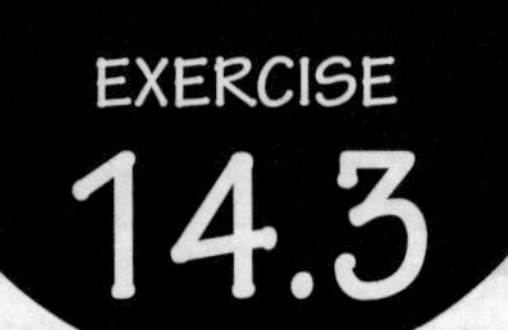

NAME: ______________________________ CLASS PERIOD: ____________

Imperfect Pies

Businesses can face problems that cause only minor dips in profit—or problems that cause complete failure. Business decisions can affect how many goods a business will produce (the supply) or how many goods customers want (the demand). Events that can't be controlled by management can also affect the supply of and the demand for goods.

Read the following scenarios to determine what problems with supply or demand Perfect Pies, Inc. might face.

Scenario 1

The pie crust supervisor burst into the boss's office, shouting "I don't know what to do about the pie crust machine! It keeps tearing the crusts."

The boss asked, "What are our options?"

The supervisor responded, "We could get it fixed, but the machine is getting old, and it's difficult to get parts. Another option is to get a new machine, but that's going to be expensive."

The boss responded, "You forgot a third option. Let's just go back to making the pie crust by hand. We don't need a machine. I've got to go now; I've got a 2:00 p.m. golf game."

Questions

If the pie company goes back to making the crusts by hand, will the supply of pies increase or decrease?

____

Is this a problem that can be controlled by management?

____

Scenario 2

"This is a disaster!" exclaimed the fillings supervisor. "There are worms in the apples. I've ordered more from the growers, but now I've been told there are worms in all of the apples. We have a worm infestation! This is terrible! Thanksgiving is right around the corner, and we aren't going to have any apples for apple pies. We're going to lose a lot of money!"

Questions

If the pie company cannot get apples without worms, will the supply of apple pies increase or decrease?

____

Is this a problem that can be controlled by management?

____

Scenario 3

"Hey, you've lost some weight!" Claire said as she saw Madison come through the door.

"Yes," said Madison excitedly, "I lost it on the Pronly diet."

"I've never heard of that diet. Tell me about it," Claire said.

Madison explained, "It's the protein-only diet. You eat meats, cheese and beans. And, most important, you never eat pies! Everybody's doing it."

Questions

If the Pronly diet becomes popular, what will happen to the demand for apple pies?

____

Is this a problem that can be controlled by management?

____

NAME: ____ CLASS PERIOD: ____________

Mutual Funds

Directions: After reading the following description of mutual funds, brainstorm with your group to complete the assignment.

To reduce the risk of loss, many investors follow a plan to diversify their holdings. Investors put their savings dollars into different kinds of investments so that possible losses in one kind are balanced by gains in another. For example, an investor might hold a combination of technology, health care, and service industry stocks. An investor might also choose blue chip stocks as well as unproven, new, growth stocks.

Mutual funds are based on the idea of diversification. A mutual fund company uses investors' money to buy a variety of stocks. Small investors can thus invest in a greater number and variety of stock than they could have done if they were to buy stocks individually. The investor gains or loses based on the total fund's performance—the gains and losses of all the individual stocks in the fund.

People who can afford to accept greater risk will often choose mutual funds that buy stock in small or medium-size companies. People who cannot afford to accept high levels of risk will choose funds that buy stock in large, stable companies and other stable assets.

Assignment

Describe the kind of people who would be uncomfortable accepting high levels of risk and would, therefore, choose a mutual fund that buys stocks of large, stable companies, providing constant, relatively small returns. Hint: Think about age, income, and financial obligations.

____

____

____

Describe the kind of people who would be willing to accept higher levels of risk in hopes of gaining a high return on their investments. Hint: Think about age, income, and financial obligations.

____

____

____

Introduction

Spending and Credit

What's more fun than shopping?

Homework? Babysitting? Cleaning your room? Probably not.

But trying on the latest fashions, checking out a terrific new video game, tasting a delicious ice cream flavor at the mall: now those are fun things to do. In fact, the whole experience of shopping has nearly replaced baseball as the national pastime.

Shopping for a bargain presents exciting challenges. You begin by checking out commercials and advertisements to compare different brands. Then you probably go from store to store to find just what you want at the best price. But even though shopping is fun, it can also be frustrating, especially if you find something you really want, but you don't have enough money to pay for it.

What can you do if you're short of cash? You might be able to use credit to buy the item now, but you'll have to pay for it eventually - and you'll probably be paying interest too.

Yes, shopping can be a pleasant Sunday afternoon adventure or a disastrous assault on your finances. It's up to you. By being a wise and sensible shopper - one who looks for the best quality and price, and who pays bills on time - you'll have the foundation for sensible money management and a good credit record. Good credit combined with rational spending habits can set you on the road to your financial well-being.

LESSON 15

Cash or Credit?

Introduction

A typical Sunday edition of the *Chicago Tribune* weighs nearly five pounds. Half of the paper contains news, features, and editorials; the other half—about 2 1/2 pounds—is advertising.

Advertising is an important component of a market economy. It attempts to increase the demand for certain goods and services by shaping people's tastes and preferences. For example, an ad that shows a famous athlete drinking a new brand of sports drink might encourage more people to buy the product. When great-looking models on a billboard are wearing designer jeans, consumers may believe buying that brand of jeans will make them just as attractive as the models.

Of course, when people respond to advertising, they may end up spending money. It might be a small amount, like $10 to download an album, or it could be hundreds of dollars for clothes, sporting goods, a computer, or an mp3 player. There's nothing wrong with spending money; in fact, consumer spending generates positive effects in the economy, including more jobs and income for workers and more taxes to support public projects.

But sometimes spending can get out of hand. Sometimes people spend more money than they actually have. One way they do this is by using credit. Credit, when handled wisely, allows a person to buy a product now, use and enjoy it, and pay for it later—often with interest. If there were no credit, most people would have difficulty saving enough to buy a house or a new car, and many students would not be able to go to college.

Just like other decisions, however, the decision to use credit involves an opportunity cost. And with credit, the opportunity cost lies in the future. When you buy that birthday present for your mom on credit, she can enjoy it right away, but you'll have to pay for it eventually. And when you do, you'll have to give up spending that money for something else you might want in order to make the payment.

LESSON 15

Vocabulary

Annual fee: The yearly charge for having a credit card.

Annual Percentage Rate (APR): The total cost of credit for one year, expressed as a percentage. The APR includes interest and other fees associated with the loan.

Credit limit: The maximum amount of credit extended to you by a bank or credit card issuer.

Finance charge: The total dollar amount you must pay for the credit you use. These charges may include interest and other fees such as a loan application fee.

Grace period: A period of time during which you are not charged interest on new purchases (if you have no outstanding balance).

Inflation: A general increase in prices.

Interest: The price of using credit.

Interest rate: The price of using credit expressed as a percentage of the amount owed.

Late fee: A penalty, in addition to interest, that is charged if payment is received after the due date.

Minimum payment: The lowest amount you must pay toward your credit balance each month.

Opportunity cost: The next-best alternative that is given up when a choice is made.

NAME: ______________________ CLASS PERIOD: __________

So Many Credit Card Offers: What's the Difference?

With your partner, examine two credit card applications. Then complete the chart below and answer the questions that follow.

	Credit Card A	Credit Card B
Annual fee		
Interest rate (APR)		
Grace period		
Minimum payment		
Late fee		
Other fees		

If you were to choose one of these credit cards, which one would it be?

____

What are the benefits of the card you chose?

____

____

What are some of the costs of the card you chose?

____

____

NAME: ______________________ CLASS PERIOD: __________

Cash or Credit? You Be the Judge

Read the four stories below and analyze each person's spending decision regarding the laptop sale advertised above.

A. Elizabeth wants to buy a new laptop computer, but she just started her baby-sitting job and she hasn't earned any money yet. She figures once she starts earning income she can save $90 a month in a savings account that earns three percent interest annually. Elizabeth learned about inflation in school. Inflation is a general increase in prices. She learned that the annual inflation rate is currently about three percent.

She decides to save her money and buy the laptop next year when she can afford to pay cash for it.

1. Assuming the price of the laptop computer increases at the rate of inflation, how much will the laptop computer cost a year from now?

(HINT: $1,000 x .03 + $1,000) ______________________

2. How much will Elizabeth put into her account in the year?

____

3. Will Elizabeth be able to buy the laptop computer?

____

4. Will Elizabeth have any money left over?

____

B. David would like to buy a laptop computer and save 20 percent during the sale. He uses his credit card to pay for it. David is counting on getting a lot of money in graduation presents from his parents' business associates. David knows that his credit card company offers a 28-day grace period, so if he pays off the whole amount, he won't owe any interest.

Sure enough, after his big party, David counts up the checks and he has $1,000! When he gets his credit card bill at the end of the month, he is able to pay the balance of $800 in full.

1. How long will it take for David to pay off the $800?

____

2. How much interest will he have to pay?

____

C. Ryan has a credit card that charges interest at an APR of 18 percent. When he spotted a sale, he wanted to take advantage of the $200 savings and buy a laptop computer at the sale price. Ryan plans to save $90 a month from his job as an office assistant in his dad's insurance business. He plans to pay the credit card company $90 every month until his bill is paid.

1. Use the chart on the next page to figure out how long it will take him to pay off his credit card debt; the first month is done for you. (HINT: Monthly interest rate is .18/12=.015.)

____

EXERCISE 15.2

NAME: ____________________ CLASS PERIOD: __________

Ryan's Credit Card Summary

A	B	C	D	E	F
No. of Months	Amount Owed	$90 paid each month	Monthly Interest Paid (B x .015)	Principal Paid (C-D)	New Balance
Month 1	$800.00	$90.00	$12.00	$78.00	$722.00
Month 2	$722.00	$90.00	$10.83	$79.17	$642.83
Month 3					
Month 4					
Month 5					
Month 6					
Month 7					
Month 8					
Month 9					
Month 10					

2. Add all the numbers in Columns C and D to find out how much Ryan ended up spending when he bought the laptop computer.

____

D. Caitlin really wants a new laptop computer, too, and the 20% off sale is very tempting, so she decides to use her credit card and buy the laptop computer now for $800.

Caitlin works once in a while for her neighbor—cleaning, baby-sitting, or mowing the lawn—but she doesn't really earn a regular income. She probably won't be able to save much money, so she plans to pay only the minimum required every month on her credit card bill.

(NOTE: The minimum payment in this example is calculated as 2.5 percent of the balance, or $10, whichever is higher. Also note that, because of rounding, calculations may vary from those found on a computer spreadsheet.)

1. Look at the chart for Caitlin's Credit Card Summary for the first 22 months and the last 17 months of her payments. The chart shows what happens when Caitlin makes only the minimum payment. Then answer the following questions.

- How many years will it take to pay for the laptop computer?

  ____

- How much will Caitlin spend for the $800 laptop computer? (Total of Column C)

  ____

- How much interest will Caitlin pay (Column D) on her purchase?

  ____

Caitlin's Credit Card Summary

A	B	C	D	E	F
No. of Months	Amount Owed	Minimum Payment (.025 x B)	Monthly Interest Paid (B x .015)	Principal Paid (C - D)	New Balance
Month 1	$800.00	$20.00	$12.00	$8.00	$792.00
Month 2	$792.00	$19.80	$11.88	$7.92	$784.08
Month 3	$784.08	$19.60	$11.76	$7.84	$776.24
Month 4	$776.24	$19.41	$11.64	$7.76	$768.48
Month 5	$768.48	$19.21	$11.53	$7.68	$760.79
Month 6	$760.79	$19.02	$11.41	$7.61	$753.18
Month 7	$753.18	$18.83	$11.30	$7.53	$745.65
Month 8	$745.65	$18.64	$11.18	$7.46	$738.20
Month 9	$738.20	$18.45	$11.07	$7.38	$730.81
Month 10	$730.81	$18.27	$10.96	$7.31	$723.51
Month 11	$723.51	$18.09	$10.85	$7.24	$716.27
Month 12	$716.27	$17.91	$10.74	$7.16	$709.11
Month 13	$709.11	$17.73	$10.64	$7.09	$702.02
Month 14	$702.02	$17.55	$10.53	$7.02	$695.00
Month 15	$695.00	$17.37	$10.42	$6.95	$688.05
Month 16	$688.05	$17.20	$10.32	$6.88	$681.17
Month 17	$681.17	$17.03	$10.22	$6.81	$674.35
Month 18	$674.35	$16.86	$10.12	$6.74	$667.61
Month 19	$667.61	$16.69	$10.02	$6.67	$660.93
Month 20	$660.93	$16.52	$9.91	$6.61	$654.33
Month 21	$654.33	$16.36	$9.81	$6.54	$647.78
Month 22	$647.78	$16.19	$9.72	$6.48	$641.30

A	B	C	D	E	F
No. of Months	Amount Owed	Minimum Payment (.025 x B)	Monthly Interest Paid (B x .015)	Principal Paid (C - D)	New Balance
Month 115	$145.29	$10.00	$2.18	$7.82	$137.47
Month 116	$137.47	$10.00	$2.06	$7.94	$129.53
Month 117	$129.53	$10.00	$1.94	$8.06	$121.47
Month 118	$121.47	$10.00	$1.82	$8.18	$113.47
Month 119	$113.47	$10.00	$1.70	$8.30	$104.99
Month 120	$104.99	$10.00	$1.57	$8.43	$96.57
Month 121	$96.57	$10.00	$1.45	$8.55	$88.02
Month 122	$88.02	$10.00	$1.32	$8.68	$79.34
Month 123	$79.34	$10.00	$1.19	$8.81	$70.53
Month 124	$70.53	$10.00	$1.06	$8.94	$61.59
Month 125	$61.59	$10.00	$0.92	$9.08	$52.51
Month 126	$52.51	$10.00	$0.79	$9.21	$43.30
Month 127	$43.30	$10.00	$0.65	$9.35	$33.95
Month 128	$33.95	$10.00	$0.51	$9.49	$24.46
Month 129	$24.46	$10.00	$0.37	$9.63	$14.82
Month 130	$14.82	$10.00	$0.22	$9.78	$5.05
Month 131	$5.05	$5.12	$0.07	$5.05	$0.00
		$1,615.49	**$815.49**		
TOTALS		**Total Payments**	**Total Interest Paid!**		

EXERCISE 15.3

NAME: ______________________ CLASS PERIOD: __________

Understanding a Credit Card Statement

ACCOUNT SUMMARY	
Account number	1234-5678-9876
Total credit line	$3,000.00
Total available credit	$2,612.00
Cash limit	$1,000.00
Cash available	$612.00
Amount past due/over limit	$0.00
Statement closing date	1/15/10
New balance	$387.49
Payment due date	2/10/10
MINIMUM PAYMENT DUE $13.00	

ACCOUNT ACTIVITY	
Previous balance	$345.55
Payments	$200.00
Other credits	$0.00
Purchases	$207.64
Cash advances	$0.00
Late fees	$29.00
FINANCE CHARGE	**$5.30**
New balance	$387.49

TRANSACTIONS

Transaction Date	Description	Reference Number	Amount
12/20/09	Super Mart Grocers	3434BR56IA787N28	$20.75
12/27/09	Zott's Gas and Go	1212SH566ER89YL7	$12.00
01/04/10	Jeff's Hardware	7070MU4747SI2433EL	$24.89
01/10/10	Mark Auto Service	5757WI78728RT999Z	$150.00

You may avoid finance charges by paying the new balance in full by 2/10/10

Explanation of Fees: $29.00 — Late fee

If you have any questions about your account, call 24 hours a day: (800) 987-6543

Mail your payment in the enclosed envelope to:

Credit Card Services
3333 Fortress Lane
Box 1110
Anywhere, U.S.A. 00001-1110

Or pay online at: www.CCSPayMyPretendBill.com

Refer to the credit card statement on the previous page to answer these questions.

1. By what date must payment on this bill be received? ____________________

2. On what date was a grocery purchase made? ____________________

3. What is the $29 fee listed under Account Activity?

____

4. Why can't a $3,500 vacation be charged to this account?

____

5. What is the total amount of purchases made this month on this card?

____

6. How much of the previous balance was paid off last month?

____

7. What is the total credit line on this credit card?

____

8. How much credit was available at the time of this statement?

____

9. How much is the card holder's finance charge this month?

____

10. Why does the card holder owe a finance charge?

____

11. Based upon this person's credit limit, purchases, payments, and fees, do you think he or she is handling credit wisely? Explain your answer.

____

NAME: ______________________ CLASS PERIOD: ____________

Rubric for Evaluating Panel Discussion

Prepare a panel discussion on credit which covers the topics listed in the table. Your presentation will be evaluated according to the criteria in the table below, using the point scale.

Topics to be covered in panel discussion	**Discussed thoroughly and accurately** 2 points	**Briefly discussed with some inaccuracies** 1 point	**Not discussed** 0 points
Advantages of using credit			
Disadvantages of using credit			
APR			
Grace period			
Annual fees			
Transaction fees (late fees)			
Minimum payment and total cost			
Interesting statistcs about credit			
Recommendations for wise credit use			
How inflation may affect decisions about use of credit			
The opportunity cost of credit			
Totals			
Grand Total of Three Columns			

LESSON 16

Establishing Credit

Introduction

Remember the fable of the boy who cried wolf? The shepherd boy made up so many stories about seeing a wolf in the pasture that when he actually did see one, no one in the village believed him or answered his cries for help. If he had been honest and trustworthy in the beginning, his story would have been accepted when he was in real trouble.

This fable also says something about what is needed in order to establish a good credit history. People who borrow money and don't return it, or who are consistently late in making payments on loans, will have a bad credit record. They will not be trusted because of their past history and will have trouble getting loans or credit cards in the future. More important, being turned down for credit can have unfortunate consequences: perhaps no college financial aid, or no new car, no house, furniture, or even an mp3 player or computer.

This lesson will help you understand the importance of establishing a good credit history. By being a responsible borrower in small things, you can develop good habits that lead to a favorable credit record. Then, when you are older, you will avoid problems when applying for a loan for big-ticket items, such as a car or a house.

Vocabulary

Collateral: Property or other valuables used as security to guarantee the repayment of a loan. The lender can claim collateral if the borrower fails to repay.

Credit bureau: A firm that collects borrowers' credit histories.

Credit report: A history of a borrower's use of credit. You should get a copy of your credit report once a year to ensure there are no mistakes.

Credit score: A score used to evaluate a borrower's credit worthiness and likelihood to repay a loan. Credit scores are based primarily on a borrower's payment history and the amount owed. Other factors used in determining credit scores include how long you have had each account, the mix of types of credit used (credit cards and loans) and factors related to any new credit account that has recently been opened.

Debt to income ratio: A measurement of how much of your income is being spent on debt. Many financial advisors suggest that you keep debt levels below 15 percent of your net income and that debt levels of 20 percent of your net income are dangerously high. This limit does not include mortgage payments.

Completed Loan Application and Credit Report - Applicant 1

Loan Application, Part A

Loan amount requested: $10,000   Length of loan: 4 years
Monthly payment: $240   Reason for loan: Buy a used car

Personal Information:
(A) Applicant's name: James Paul Anderson   Date of birth: 9-2-82
(S) Spouse's name: Judith Rice Anderson   Date of birth: 9-29-83

Marital status (please mark one): ☐ single ☑ married

Address: 704 Houser Street   **Social security #:** (A) 002-92-8976
City: Leslietown   (S) 202-35-7653
State: VA   **Zip:** 24523
Phone: (703) 927-0909

Dependents:	**Relationship:**	**Age:**
Sean Stuart Anderson	son	6 mos.

Education (record only your highest level of education attained):
(A) High school diploma   (S) High school diploma

Employment (list only the current jobs held by you or your spouse):
(A) Construction laborer   (S) Homemaker
Building Contractors, Inc.

Household gross annual employment income: $40,800
Approximate net annual employment income: $34,350
Other income: none
Monthly net income: $2,863

Do you: ☐ own ☑ rent ☐ live with others?
Monthly mortgage or rent expense: $655

Adapted from *Personal Finance Economics, 6–8: Money in the Middle*

Loan Application, Part B

Current Loans Outstanding (List the lender, loan type, balance owed, monthly payment, and remaining period of loan):

1) Seventh Bank	Personal loan	$1,960	$180	11 mos.
2) You Buy It Now	TV/furniture	$2,000	$ 90	32 mos.

Credit cards (List the name of the lender, type of card, current balance outstanding, typical monthly payment):

1) Seventh Bank	VIDA Card	$2,500	$62

References (You must list in the designated order: your current employer, previous employer, and nearest relative not living with you):

1) Samantha Sternwell	Building Contractors, Inc	(703) 927-7623
2) Jason Briddet	Skyscrapers, Incorporated	(703) 937-8354
3) Martha S. Anderson	Leslietown, VA	(703) 927-0098

Purpose of loan: We would like to buy a newer car. Our current car is not reliable and needs repair. We would like to borrow $10,000 for four years and think we could afford a monthly payment of $240.

Credit Report

James P. and Judith Anderson

Financial Information	**Item**	**Balance/Value**
Checking accounts(s):	Seventh Bank	$3,000
Savings accounts(s):	Seventh Bank	$2,000
Investments:	none	
Real estate:	none	

Reference Information

Landlord:	Always pay rent on time. Excellent tenant. Good neighbor to others in building.
Seventh Bank:	New customer but timely with payments. They took out a personal loan last month, have had their credit card for six months, and have been paying the minimum on their balance each month.
You Buy It Now:	Recently opened their account. Timely payments so far.

Completed Loan Application and Credit Report - Applicant 2

Loan Application, Part A

Loan amount requested: $38,000 Length of loan: 5 years
Monthly payment: $773.00 Reason for loan: Buy a sporty new car

Personal Information:
(A) Applicant's name: Joey Deligh Date of birth: 1-5-80
(S) Spouse's name: ____ Date of birth: ____

Marital status (please mark one): ☑ single ☐ married

Address: 9191 Edgemare Drive **Social security #:** (A) 778-90-6732
(S) ____
City: Leslietown
State: VA **Zip:** 24523
Phone: (703) 927-1112

Dependents:	**Relationship:**	**Age:**
none		

Education (record only your highest level of education attained):
(A) Bachelor of Science in Marketing (S)
University of Leslietown

Employment (list only the current jobs held by you or your spouse):
(A) Advertising Executive (S)
Billboards Galore

Household gross annual employment income:	$91,100
Approximate net annual employment income:	$64,320
Other income:	$ 2,000
Monthly net income:	$ 5,527

Do you: ☑ own ☐ rent ☐ live with others?
Monthly mortgage or rent expense: $1,054

Loan Application, Part B

Current Loans Outstanding (List the lender, loan type, balance owed, monthly payment, and remaining period of loan):

1) Sixth Bank	Personal business	$ 9,000	$500	57 mos.
2) Sixth Bank	Auto	$ 286	$290	1 mos.
3) Wildcat Lenders	Education	$19,500	$348	67 mos.

Credit cards (List the name of the lender, type of card, current balance outstanding, typical monthly payment):

1) Sixth Bank	VIDA Card	$8,500	$125
2) Sixth Bank	Charge-It-Meter	$5,000	$ 75

References (You must list in the designated order: your current employer, previous employer, and nearest relative not living with you):

1) Hayward Stephens	Billboard Galore	(803) 937-9998
2) No previous employer		
3) Ronald Deligh	Winston, CA	(909) 843-1121

Purpose of loan: I would like to buy a new car. I am about to pay off my current car and don't want it anymore. If I borrow $38,000 for five years, my payment would be $733 per month and I could get a sporty new car.

Credit Report

Joey Deligh

Financial Information	**Item**	**Balance/Value**
Checking accounts(s):	Sixth Bank	$ 600
Savings accounts(s):	Sixth Bank	$ 1,200
Investments:	IMF Mutual Funds	$ 6,000
Real estate:	9191 Edgemare Dr.	$12,000*

*Value of home less than what is owed on its mortgage.

Reference Information

Mortgage Holder:	Frequently late making payments. Currently behind one monthly mortgage payment.
Sixth Bank:	Has two outstanding loans and two credit cards with our bank. Has been late with payments in the past. Currently up to date with both loan payments. However, credit cards are at their maximum credit limit and he has been paying the minimum payment on balance owed.
Wildcat Lenders:	Always pays on time.
Ronald Deligh (father):	Is willing to co-sign on a loan.

Completed Loan Application and Credit Report - Applicant 3

Loan Application, Part A

Loan amount requested: $25,000 Length of loan: 7 years
Monthly payment: $340.00 Reason for loan: Buy a boat

Personal Information:
(A) Applicant's name: Claudette Ransdia Date of birth: 12-08-63
(S) Spouse's name: Landon H. Ransdia Date of birth: 8-01-64
Marital status (please mark one): ☐ single ☑ married

Address: 5608 Uptown Street **Social security #:** (A) 209-96-1746
(S) 207-33-7330
City: Leslietown
State: VA **Zip:** 24533
Phone: (703) 937-1990

Dependents:	**Relationship:**	**Age:**
S. Olivia Ransdia	daughter	16
John S. Ransdia	son	13
Erin E. Ransdia	daughter	12

Education (record only your highest level of education attained):
(A) Juris Doctor (S) Master of Arts in Education
James Madison University University of Wyoming

Employment (list only the current jobs held by you or your spouse):
(A) Attorney (S) Teacher
Jones, Barnett, & Cline Leslie County Middle School
Attorneys at Law

Household gross annual employment income: $168,000
Approximate net annual employment income: $118,332
Other income: $ 2,000
Monthly net income: $ 10,028
Do you: ☑ own ☐ rent ☐ live with others?
Monthly mortgage or rent expense: $1,500

Loan Application, Part B

Current Loans Outstanding (List the lender, loan type, balance owed, monthly payment, and remaining period of loan):

1) Leslietown Bank	Auto	$ 4,300	$145	33 mos.
2) Leslietown Bank	Auto	$ 8,000	$247	38 mos.
3) Leslietown Bank	College	$21,000	$293	93 mos.
4) Leslietown Bank	Motor Home	$26,000	$587	57 mos.

Credit cards (List the name of the lender, type of card, current balance outstanding, typical monthly payment):

1) Leslietown Bank	VIDA Card	$250	in full
2) Leslietown Bank	Charge-It-Meter	$750	in full
3) AmeriPlan Bank	Explorers	$6,750	$1,000

References (You must list in the designated order: your current employer, previous employer, and nearest relative not living with you):

1) (A) Reginald Jones	Jones, Barnette & Cline Attorneys at Law	(703) 591-4325
1) (S) Janis Franken	Leslie County Schools	(703) 927-4443
2) No previous employer		
3) Mia Ransdia	Band, KY	(502) 224-2224

Purpose of loan: We would like to buy a boat. We vacation every summer at the lake and the kids like to water ski. We would like to borrow $25,000 for seven years and think we could afford the monthly paymeny of $340.

Credit Report

Landon H. and Claudette Ransdia

Financial Information	Item	Balance/Value
Checking accounts(s):	Leslietown Bank	$ 2,500
Savings accounts(s):	Leslietown Bank	$ 1,000
	AmeriPlan Fund	$ 4,000
Investments:	AmeriPlan Fund	$22,000
	Digtiec Corp. Stock	$16,000
Real estate:	5608 Uptown St.	$67,000*

*Value of home less than what is owed on its mortgage.

Reference Information

Mortgage Holder:	Always pays mortgage on time. We have been doing business with the couple for 20 years.
Leslietown Bank:	Currently, we have four loans and two credit cards with the applicants. Have never been late with a payment in 20 years.
AmeriPlan Bank:	Monthly credit card balance fluctuates between $8,000 and $0 each year. Highest balances in late summer and the lowest in early spring.

Completed Loan Application and Credit Report - Applicant 4

Loan Application, Part A

Loan amount requested: $12,000 Length of loan: 5 years
Monthly payment: $239.00 Reason for loan: Purchase a motor home

Personal Information:
(A) Applicant's name: Mr. Rhett Willis Date of birth: 11-14-65
(S) Spouse's name: ________ Date of birth: ________

Marital status (please mark one): ☑ single ☐ married

Address: 14 Town Street **Social security #:** (A) 402-48-3278
City: Leslietown (S)
State: VA **Zip:** 40533
Phone: (883) 927-3345

Dependents:	Relationship:	Age:
Mary Jo Willis	daughter*	11
Melanie Willis	daughter*	9

*Mr. Willis's daughters live with their mother, who receives $450 in child support each month from their dad.

Education (record only your highest level of education attained):
(A) Associate's Degree (S)
Leslietown Community College

Employment (list only the current jobs held by you or your spouse):
(A) General Electrician (S)
Self-employed

Household gross annual employment income: $48,000
Approximate net annual employment income: $38,076
Other income: $ 10
Monthly net income: $ 3,174
Do you: ☐ own ☑ rent ☐ live with others?
Monthly mortgage or rent expense: $871

Loan Application, Part B

Current Loans Outstanding (List the lender, loan type, balance owed, monthly payment, and remaining period of loan):

1) Leslietown Bank   Auto $ 9,000 $250   60 mos.

Credit cards (List the name of the lender, type of card, current balance outstanding, typical monthly payment):

1) Our Town Bank   VIDA Card $2,000 $55

Purpose of loan: I would like to buy a used motor home which is priced at $12,000. I think I can pay $239 a month over 5 years for the motor home.

Credit Report

Mr. Rhett Willis

Financial Information	Item	Balance/Value
Checking accounts(s):	Sixth Bank	$1,250
	Sixth Bank	$2,900
Savings accounts(s):	Sixth Bank	$600
Investments:	none	
Real estate:	none	

Reference Information

Landlord:	Mr. Willis has been a tenant for four years. He always pays his rent, although he has been late a couple times in the last six months.
Our Town Bank:	Long-standing customer. Credit cards have outstanding balances, but he has made payments on them in a timely fashion.
Leslietown Bank:	Always pays auto loan on a timely basis.
Clarence Mims:	Mr. Willis was a faithful and dedicated employee for 15 years before he resigned six months ago to start his own business. He buys equipment and supplies from us and always pays on time.
Thomas Willis (father):	Cannot co-sign on a loan. He is elderly and has a limited, fixed income.

NAME: ______________________________ CLASS PERIOD: __________

Applicant Summary Sheet

What does the loan application and credit report tell you about the following:

A. The applicant's character: ______________________________

____

____

____

B. The applicant's capacity: ______________________________

____

____

____

C. The applicant's collateral: ______________________________

____

____

____

D. Percent of income currently spent on debt (other than mortgage payments)? __________
(Hint: debt payments of 15 percent of net income are usually manageable; debt payments of 20 percent or more can be dangerously high.)

E. Percent of income spent on debt if you include the new loan payment? __________

Would you lend money to this applicant? Yes ___ No ___

Explain why or why not: ______________________________

____

____

Character Counts (So Do Capacity, Collateral, and Credit Scores)

Character: You may be a fine, upstanding citizen, but if you want to borrow money, you are going to have to prove it to lenders. When you are being evaluated for a loan, the lender will review your credit history as shown on your credit report. Your credit report is a detailing of the credit you are currently being granted, the credit you have been granted in the past, and how well you maintained that credit. The lender will review your credit report and credit history, watching for the following:

- Your bill-paying history: who has extended you credit in the past and your record of paying your debts on time.
- Your history of managing other finances, such as a checking account.
- Your identification and employment information, including your income, whether or not you own a home, how long you have lived at your current residence, and how long you have been at your current job.
- Your public record information, such as bankruptcies, foreclosures, and tax liens.

Young people seeking to borrow money often will discover one little problem with demonstrating their character: they can't get credit without a credit history, and they can't get a credit history without someone offering them credit. Okay, it's actually a big problem. However, there are ways to solve it. A person can begin to build a credit history in the following ways:

- Open a checking or savings account. Maintaining a checking or savings account in a responsible manner indicates stability and good money-management habits. Don't bounce a check!
- Establish a department store credit card. Department stores may allow you to open an account with a low credit limit.
- Obtain a small starter loan or credit card. Consider using a savings account as collateral for a small loan at a bank. Or ask your bank officer for a "starter" credit card, which has a low credit limit or can be secured by the cash in a savings account. Borrow only what you can comfortably repay. If you obtain a credit card, pay the entire balance on time, each month!
- Have your utilities and phone billed in your name. Paying your bills on time is an indication that you are creditworthy.
- Get a co-signer for a loan. Ask a friend or family member to co-sign a loan for you. Be sure to pay the loan off as agreed. If you don't pay, your co-signer will have to pay.

Capacity: The lender will want to know if the borrower can afford to repay the loan. To make this determination, the lender will review the following:

- Income from all sources—to make sure the borrower has enough income to make the payments.

- Other assets, such as investments and money in savings accounts that can be liquidated if necessary to make a payment.
- Current debts: Many financial advisors consider 20 percent of your take-home pay, or net monthly income, to be the maximum you should spend on consumer debt. (This amount does not include mortgage payments.) A limit of 15 percent of net monthly income is a safer level of debt.
- Net worth (the difference between everything you own and everything you owe).

Collateral: Perhaps you've heard the complaint that banks only give loans to people who don't need them. In other words, some loan applicants are told they can't get a loan because they have no assets (things of value). Their response? "If I had assets, I wouldn't need a loan!" This is an exaggeration. Lenders want to know that borrowers have something of value—collateral—that could be sold to repay the loan just in case the borrower defaults (doesn't repay). The lender will review the following:

- The fair market value of the collateral (a car, a house).
- Insurance on collateral—to repair or replace it if it is damaged.

Often the collateral for a loan is the item for which the borrower took out the loan. For instance, if you borrow money to purchase a car, the lender will use the car as collateral. If you don't make your payments, the lender will take possession of the car. You must carry insurance on the car in case it is damaged. That way, if the car is damaged, your insurance will pay for the repair, and the value of the collateral (the repaired car) is maintained. Even if the car is damaged beyond repair, the insurance company will pay the value of the car, and the lender will not lose the loan money.

Lenders request information regarding the three "Cs" (character, capacity, and collateral) to determine the level of risk they will be assuming by lending money to the applicant. Risk is uncertainty of repayment. The higher the risk, the higher the interest rate. Keep in mind that, if the borrower fails to repay the loan, the lender's profits will be reduced. A person with a very poor credit history may only be able to get credit at a very high rate of interest.

Credit Scores: Lenders also use credit scores to make decisions about loans. Credit scores are based on credit histories. Credit reporting agencies summarize the information they have in their report of your credit history by scoring it, using a statistical model. Your credit score serves as another measure of your credit risk. One commonly used model (FICO) was developed by Fair, Isaac and Company, Inc. FICO scores range between 350 and 850—the higher the number, the better the score and the more likely the borrower will be granted a loan at a low interest rate. Credit scores are also used by insurance agencies and employers to make decisions. A very good place to get your credit report is the Annual Credit Report web site: www.annualcreditreport.com.

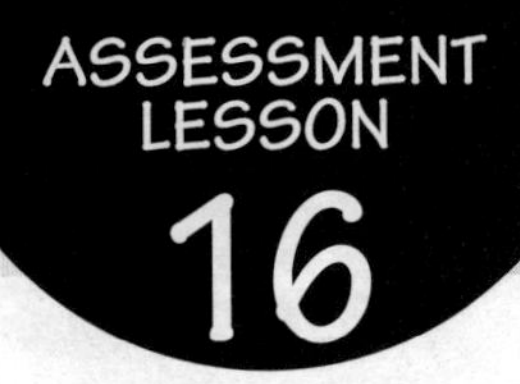

NAME: ______________________________ CLASS PERIOD: __________

Using Your Evaluation Skills

You are the loan officer for Sixth Bank in Leslietown. You have received a completed loan application from one of your customers, Rhett Willis. Evaluate the loan application for Rhett Willis found in Exercise 16.1D. Then complete the following:

What does the application from Rhett Willis tell you about the following:

A. His character? ______________________________

B. His capacity? ______________________________

C. His collateral? ______________________________

D. Percent of income currently spent on debt? ____________________
(Hint: debt payments of 15 percent of net income are usually manageable; debt payments of 20 percent or more can be dangerously high.)

E. Percent of income spent on debt with new loan payment? ____________

Would you lend money to this individual? Yes _______ No_______

Explain why or why not:

____

____

____

____

Comparison Shopping

Introduction

In May 2010, the Big Game Lottery paid out more than $300 million to two winners. After taxes, each received about $55 million. Chances are that with that much money, the winners won't be clipping store coupons or checking newspaper advertisements for the best deal on a tube of toothpaste. But even with all that money, the winners might still shop around for a good price on a sports car, a designer wardrobe, or a piece of property on the French Riviera.

The truth is, no matter how rich or poor people are, they still need to compare prices. And for average people—those who have tight budgets and count their pennies—comparison shopping is an essential skill that can pay off in big savings and more choices. Just think about it.

Let's say there are two hot dog stands near your school, Jo's and Sam's. The hot dogs and other items at both stands are of equal quality. Jo charges $2.25 for a hot dog; Sam charges $2.75. It's only 50 cents difference; no big deal, right? WRONG. If you have a hot dog for lunch every day for the three years you're in middle school, you'll save $270 by buying your lunch at Jo's instead of Sam's. Simply by being a wise shopper, you'll have extra money to buy a few music CDs, a pair of athletic shoes and some new jeans, or maybe a few video games.

This lesson will demonstrate that wise consumers compare prices before they buy. It will show how to shop for the best deal and how to calculate whether the 14-ounce or 22-ounce box of Frosty Fire Hydrant Cereal is the best bargain. By being a careful shopper, one who evaluates prices and products, you can improve your chances of buying quality goods and services at prices that you can afford.

Vocabulary

Cost/benefit analysis: Comparing advantages and disadvantages in order to make a decision.

Deceptive practices: What a business person may do to fool a customer in order to sell the customer a good or service. Misleading prices, bait and switch, and false advertising are examples of deceptive practices. These practices are not legal and are unethical.

Decision-making grid: A tool used to help people compare items so that they can make a wise consumer decision.

Opportunity cost: The next-best alternative that is given up when a choice is made.

EXERCISE 17.1

NAME: ________________________________ CLASS PERIOD: __________

A Wise Person Once Said ...

Write your impression of the meaning of the two adages given below.

"Penny wise, pound foolish."

"A penny saved is a penny earned."

Do the two statements agree with each other, or are they contradictory? Explain.

____

____

____

____

____

____

____

____

____

____

____

____

____

EXERCISE 17.2

NAME: ______________________ CLASS PERIOD: __________

Major Steps in Deciding What to Buy

1. Identify what you want. (Our team's product assignment is...)

____

____

2. Determine how much you can spend. (Our budget for this item is...)

____

____

3. Find out what products or services are available in your price range. (Use store ads or visit websites.) List these alternatives below and along the left side of the decision-making grid.

____

____

4. Choose the features you would most like to have. (List the features you definitely want along the top of the grid. You might want to have a list of "optional" features, which you could also put along the top of the grid. In addition, your group may want to simply note that some alternatives are preferred because they do not have features that you do not want.)

5. Use the decision-making grid on the next page to analyze the alternatives.

6. Watch for hidden costs. (List any costs for necessary accessories; list any sales taxes or charges.)

7. Make your choice.

Definitely want: ______________________

Optional: ______________________

Do not want: ______________________

NAME: ______________________ CLASS PERIOD: __________

Decision-Making Grid

Features ➡ / ⬇ Alternatives						Total Points

EXERCISE 17.3

Poor Mrs. Amos

CAST OF CHARACTERS		
Narrator	**Salesman**	**Mrs. Amos**

Narrator: Mrs. Amos is a widow. She lives on a fixed retirement income. The salesman works on commission, meaning he gets a percentage of each sale he makes. The salesman is using a sales technique often reported to consumer protection agencies by consumers, particularly by older people. In this technique, the salesman applies pressure and tries to make the consumer feel foolish if he or she doesn't make the purchase.

The telephone rings. Mrs. Amos answers. The salesman speaks.

Salesman: Good afternoon, Mrs. Amos. How are you this afternoon?

Mrs. Amos: I'm fine thank you.

Salesman: That's great news, Mrs. Amos. I hope you're staying out of the heat.

Mrs. Amos: Oh, I'm trying.

Salesman: Well, Mrs. Amos. I'm with Lovely Lawns. We've been in your neighborhood lately working on many of your neighbors' lawns. We've noticed that your lawn has large, brown patches, which could indicate pest infestation or fungus. If you don't address this problem soon, you will probably lose your entire lawn.

Mrs. Amos: What should I do?

Salesman: Well, Mrs. Amos, here's the good news. We can take care of that problem for you. Our technician will come by your home and spray our patented pesticide and fungicide. Your lawn will be full and green again in no time.

Mrs. Amos: How much will it cost?

Salesman: Well, that's the best news yet. One application costs $48, but we will do four applications throughout the summer for only $150. That's a saving to you, Mrs. Amos, of $42.

Mrs. Amos: I suppose I could have one treatment.

Salesman: I wouldn't recommend that, Mrs. Amos. We do our best to get your problem cleared up, but the treatment is only effective when it is applied four times.

Mrs. Amos: I'm afraid I can't afford more treatments than one.

Salesman: Oh, Mrs. Amos. You can't afford not to take care of this problem. After all, you don't want to be known on your block as the house with the sloppy yard.

Mrs. Amos: Well, I certainly don't want that. But I don't know how I'll be able to afford $150.

Salesman: Mrs. Amos. I completely understand. That's why we will offer you the opportunity to make installment payments for just a small fee.

Mrs. Amos: How much would the payments be?

Salesman: Well, for you, Mrs. Amos, we'll simply divide your cost into five easy payments.

Mrs. Amos: Well, I don't know. This seems like a large expense. I'm on a fixed income.

Salesman: We have many retirees as customers, Mrs. Amos. They can't be expected to do this kind of work themselves.

Mrs. Amos: I still don't know if I should do this.

Salesman: Mrs. Amos, if you don't mind my saying, I don't know how you can pass this up. What will your neighbors think of you if your yard becomes even worse? It's already looking pretty bad.

Mrs. Amos: Well, I guess I'll do it then.

Salesman: Mrs. Amos, you've made the right decision. We'll be out tomorrow to begin the treatments. Please hold the line so that we may make a tape-recorded verification of your purchase.

Narrator: Mrs. Amos verified the sale and began the treatment. She later began receiving her installment invoices charging one-fifth of the fee plus a 20 percent interest rate.

THE END

EXERCISE 17.3

NAME: ______________________________ CLASS PERIOD: __________

Questions

1. What tactics did the salesman use to convince Mrs. Amos to sign up for the service?

____

____

2. If Mrs. Amos was uncomfortable with the salesman's tactics, what should she have done?

____

____

3. Why did Mrs. Amos stay on the phone and ultimately buy the service?

____

____

The Worm Has Turned

CAST OF CHARACTERS			
Salesman	**Tina Allen**	**Mr. Allen**	**Sales Manager**

Salesman: Hi, I'm Steve Swank. What can I do for you?

Tina Allen: I'm interested in the 2002 XYZ on your lot. What can you tell me about it?

Salesman: Oh, that's a nice one. I guess you just recently got your driver's license. Am I right?

Mr. Allen: Yes, Tina just got her license. She'll need a car to get back and forth to school. We simply have too many people and not enough cars.

Salesman: Boy, I know how that goes. I have three teenagers myself. Is this your first driver?

Mr. Allen: Yeah, Tina's our first.

Salesman: Well your little girl really knows her cars, doesn't she? She's picked the peach of the lot.

Tina Allen: *(slightly exasperated)* Could you tell us a little about the car?

Salesman: Certainly. I see in the file that it has 160,000 miles on it. Those were all highway miles, Tina. May I call you Tina? [He doesn't wait for an answer, but continues his sales pitch.] The previous owner never had a bit of trouble with it. It is loaded with options, too. You can see the great shape it's in.

Tina Allen: Could you tell me your asking price?

Salesman: Well, Tina, we've listed it for $5,000, but it's been on our lot for over a week now, and we like to turn our inventory over much more frequently than that. We have very strict standards for the used cars we will place on our lot, so they usually go very fast. As a matter of fact, I had a customer who was very interested in this car in here just yesterday. He said he would be stopping back later today.

Tina Allen: $5,000 is a little out of my price range. Could you do anything for us?

Salesman: Gee, I don't know, Tina. With that customer coming back in this afternoon, and all, I might be doing myself damage by coming down on the price. But, I like you. And I have teenagers myself. I know how important it is to be seen in a hot car, am I right? [The salesman winks at Mr. Allen.] I'll tell you what. I'll come down to $4,800.

Tina Allen: That's still a little high. Could you bring the price down to $4,200?

Salesman: Wow! That would certainly put us at a loss. I can't see any way for us to come down that low for this fine car.

Tina Allen: Well, $4,200 is all I have budgeted for a car. I can't go any higher.

Salesman: I see your dilemma. And I like you two. Let me go ask my manager. But I've got to warn you. He's going to think I'm nuts for even suggesting this price.

The salesman meets with the manager in the corner of the room. The two act as though they are arguing over the price. The salesman comes back to the desk.

Salesman: Mr. Allen, Tina, I tried. He would only come down to $4,500. That's his final offer. Even at that price, we're losing money on this car. He thinks I'm crazy. I had to pull in some favors for this one. But, as I told him, you're nice people who need a car, and that's why we're in business. We figure you'll tell your friends that you got a good deal here.

Tina Allen: That's still above my budget.

Salesman: Tina, we can certainly work out a payment plan to fit your budget. Don't think of it as $4,500. Think of it as only $125 a month. You can certainly afford that, can't you Tina?

Tina Allen: For how many months?

Salesman: Only 60.

Tina Allen: That's a long time. The car might not even last that long.

NAME: ______________________________ CLASS PERIOD: __________

Salesman: I don't see why not. It's been very well maintained. You know, my son's friend drives one of these, and he has 250,000 miles on it. It runs like a top. He's never had a day of trouble.

Mr. Allen: Well, I don't know.

Salesman: Mr. Allen, Tina, I can't tell you which way you should go on this. All I can say is that this is one nice vehicle, and I have a customer ready to buy it this afternoon.

Tina Allen: Well, I guess we'll have to leave it for your other customer. Thanks for your time. Good-bye.

THE END

Questions

1. In what ways did the salesman try to get Tina and Mr. Allen to see him as a friend?

____

____

2. In what ways did the salesman try to push Tina and her dad to buy the car?

____

____

3. Did you think Tina was going to buy the car?

____

____

4. Do you think Tina did the right thing?

____

____

Comparison Shopping

Comparison shopping is the process of considering prices and features of similar products before making a decision to buy. The more expensive or complex an item, the more a smart shopper will want to compare a variety of options before choosing one.

Comparison shopping must take into account a variety of factors such as differences in features, sizes, product quality and performance, price, and service agreements.

Advantages of Comparison Shopping

- You can save money, since prices for the same or similar products may vary dramatically from place to place.
- You may be able to get more features or value for the same amount of money.
- You may buy a better quality product that will last longer or perform better.
- You can learn about options and products you weren't aware of before.
- You will feel more secure that your money was spent wisely.

Disadvantages of Comparison Shopping

- Comparison shopping takes time, which could be used in may other ways.
- Comparison shopping may cost money—e.g., for telephone calls or gas used to visit different stores.
- The savings from comparative shopping, especially for lower-priced items, may be less than the cost of your time, gas, or other expenses.

Requirements for Comparison Shopping

- Access to reliable information.
- Time to check with a variety of vendors and to wait for sales, special selling seasons, or inventory closeouts.
- The money to purchase an item quickly if a tremendous opportunity arises.

Liar, Liar, Pants on Fire

Deceptive advertising. Producers always want to present their products in the best light. Some advertisements may contain out-and-out falsehoods, while others simply may not present the whole story. The best advice is this: if it seems too good to be true, it probably is! Toothpaste advertisements may promise whiter teeth in 30 days. How, exactly, is that comparison made? How often must you use the toothpaste in order to achieve the promised results? Won't most toothpastes whiten teeth? When the packaging shows a statement that "9 out of 10 dentists recommend this Brand X," does it mean they actually recommended Brand X or does it mean they recommended the ingredients in Brand X (which are the exact same ingredients in a dozen other brands)?

Bait and switch. While seeking information by reading through store ads, you will often come across some mighty good bargains, usually presented on the front page. Most often these are perfectly legitimate sales designed to bring your attention to the store. However, some companies may engage in an illegal practice called "bait and switch," when the quantities of the sale item are low or maybe not available at the store at all. The salesperson will apologize for the unavailability of the sale item but direct the consumer's attention to a much nicer, more expensive, item offered at a similar discount. The seller is "baiting" the consumer by offering the terrific sale item and then "switching" the consumer's attention to another, more expensive, product. The consumer, already at the store and ready to make a purchase, will often buy the alternative item. He or she may later discover that the item purchased was available at a lower price elsewhere.

Deceptive pricing. Although a store cannot legally claim that the price of a product has been reduced if it hasn't been, it can use other terminology that deceives the consumer into thinking that the item is being offered at a lower price. For instance, some stores may cover the original shelf tag with a brightly colored tag stating "Special Value" or "In-store Special." The store isn't saying that this price is lower than the retail price, but the implication to the consumer is that the price for the good has been reduced. Here's a tip: pull the colorful tag aside and observe the regular price of the good. You might find that the prices are identical.

NAME: ________________________ CLASS PERIOD: __________

Major Steps in a Purchase Decision

1. Identify what you want.

____

____

2. Determine how much you can spend.

____

____

3. Find out what products or services are available in your price range. (Use store ads or visits, visit web sites. List these alternatives along the left side of your grid.)

____

____

4. Choose the features you would most like to have. (List the features you definitely want. You may also wish to identify optional features that you would like as well as any features you definitely do not want. List the features that you definitely want and those that are optional along the top of your grid.)

5. Use the decision-making grid to help you make your decision.

6. Watch for hidden costs. (List any costs for necessary accessories; list any sales taxes or charges.)

7. Make your choice.

Definitely want: ______________________________

Optional: ______________________________

Do not want: ______________________________

NAME: ______________________ CLASS PERIOD: __________

Decision-Making Grid

Features ➡ / ⬇ Alternatives						Total Points